C. S. LEWIS'S
DANGEROUS IDEA

A Philosophical Defense
of Lewis's Argument
from Reason

Victor Reppert

InterVarsity Press
Downers Grove, Illinois

To the memory of my father, Jarrot F. Reppert,
who taught me how to ask questions and look for answers

Born December 14, 1916
Died February 14, 2002

InterVarsity Press
P.O. Box 1400, Downers Grove, IL 60515-1426
World Wide Web: www.ivpress.com
E-mail: mail@ivpress.com

InterVarsity Press® is the book-publishing division of InterVarsity Christian Fellowship/USA®, a student movement active on campus at hundreds of universities, colleges and schools of nursing in the United States of America, and a member movement of the International Fellowship of Evangelical Students. For information about local and regional activities, write Public Relations Dept., InterVarsity Christian Fellowship/USA, 6400 Schroeder Rd., P.O. Box 7895, Madison, WI 53707-7895, or visit the IVCF website at <www.ivcf.org>.

Scripture quotations, unless otherwise noted, are from the New Revised Standard Version of the Bible, copyright 1989 by the Division of Christian Education of the National Council of the Churches of Christ in the USA. Used by permission. All rights reserved.

Cover design: Cindy Kiple

ISBN 0-8308-2732-3

Printed in the United States of America ∞

Library of Congress Cataloging-in-Publication Data

Reppert, Victor, 1953-
   C.S. Lewis's dangerous idea: a philosophical defense of Lewis's
argument from reason / Victor Reppert.
     p. cm.
Includes bibliographical references and index.
   ISBN 0-8308-2732-3 (pbk.: alk. paper)
   1. Lewis, C. S. (Clive Staples), 1898-1963. 2. Faith and reason.
I. Title.
   BX5199.L53R47 2003
   212'.1—dc21

                                                                2003010874

| P | 18 | 17 | 16 | 15 | 14 | 13 | 12 | 11 | 10 | 9 | 8 | 7 | 6 | 5 | 4 | 3 | 2 | 1 |
| Y | 17 | 16 | 15 | 14 | 13 | 12 | 11 | 10 | 09 | 08 | 07 | 06 | 05 | 04 | 03 |

Contents

Preface

A FEW YEARS AGO DANIEL DENNETT wrote a book entitled *Darwin's Dangerous Idea*. In it he contrasted two types of explanations: skyhooks and cranes. A skyhook is a mind-first explanation that in the last analysis is purposive and intentional. A crane, on the other hand, makes the explanation a feature of the system that in the last analysis is a product of the mindless system of physics and chemistry. For example, if we said that your heart is in the right place because God selected that place as the optimal location for a blood pump, that would employ a skyhook. If we were to say that creatures that didn't have their hearts in the right place didn't survive long enough to pass on their genes, that would be to employ a crane. Darwin's dangerous idea, for Dennett, is that in our coming to understand the world we live in, cranes are the only acceptable kinds of explanations, and skyhooks are to be avoided. The significance of Darwin's theory, according to Dennett, is that for the first time it seemed possible to explain a lot of things without the previously needed skyhooks, and it showed us how the whole job could be done with cranes instead. Indeed this position has become orthodoxy in such varied disciplines as evolutionary biology, cognitive science and artificial intelligence, and I would say, in Anglo-American philosophy in general over the past fifty or so years.

C. S. Lewis's dangerous idea, by contrast, is that the attempt to account for the world entirely in terms of cranes overlooks something very important: the world thus analyzed has to have scientists in it.

And scientists draw their conclusions from evidence, and in so doing they engage in rational inference. But can rational inference itself be genuinely accounted for in terms of cranes? Lewis's contention was that it could not, that if you tried to account for the activity of reasoning as a byproduct of a fundamentally nonpurposive system, you end up describing something that cannot be genuinely called reasoning. If Darwin's dangerous idea is a true explanation of how Darwin got his dangerous idea, then the idea cannot possibly be the intellectual monument that Dennett supposes it to be.

The main source for this argument of Lewis's is the third chapter of his book *Miracles: A Preliminary Study*, although he uses the argument in other works, especially articles found in *Christian Reflections* and *God in the Dock*.

Although this book is about Lewis's idea and not about Lewis himself, it seems to me that there has been some reluctance to take Lewis seriously as a philosophical thinker, and I address this issue in chapter one. Part of the problem seems to be the attempt to resolve philosophical issues with biographical evidence from Lewis's life, a kind of ad hominem argument that inhibits serious consideration of Lewis as a thinker. In chapter two I address the question of what apologetic arguments can be expected to accomplish and defend a model I call critical rationalism, according to which we can consider an argument successful if it provides rational support for its conclusion, even though that support need not persuade all reasonable persons. In the third chapter I present Lewis's argument against naturalism, giving Elizabeth Anscombe's criticisms of the argument as initially presented and showing how Lewis responded to those criticisms in his revision of the argument. In chapter four I isolate several aspects of rational inference, and develop seven versions of the argument from reason based on these aspects. In chapter five I argue that these aspects of rational inference require us to admit purposive explanations as basic explanations. Chapter six considers what I call the inadequacy objection, according to which, if reasoning cannot be explained in naturalistic terms, it does no good to explain it in terms of theism either, because theistic explanations are not real explanations. I maintain, by contrast, that while explanations in terms of souls or in terms of God do lack some of the characteristics of standard scientific explanations, they nonetheless are genuine explanations.

I would like to thank various people for helping me with this book project. Deserving special mention in this regard are William Hasker, Jason Pratt, Tim Erdel, J. P. Moreland, Dennis Monokroussos, Keith Parsons, Bill Vallicella, Darek Barefoot, Richard Carrier, Jim Lippard, Ed Babinski and Jason Baeh. I would hasten to add that at least some of these people are going to disagree with a lot that I have to say. This project is a successor to my doctoral dissertation at the University of Illinois at Urbana-Champaign, entitled *Physical Causes and Rational Belief: A Problem for Materialism* (1989), and so I would like to thank committee members Robert Wengert and Robert McKim, and especially committee chairman Hugh Chandler. Most of all, I would like to thank my wife, Anne, and daughters, Sarah and Nanette, for encouraging me to write this book and supporting me throughout the process of writing it.

Taking C. S. Lewis Seriously

APOLOGETICS AND THE PERSONAL HERESY

ONE OF THE FIRST PHILOSOPHICAL ARGUMENTS I ever encountered was C. S. Lewis's argument, found in his book *Miracles*, that naturalism is self-refuting because it is inconsistent with the validity of reasoning.[1] The argument fascinated me, and as a young Christian I never missed a chance to present it in discussions with skeptics. I later discovered that this argument was the subject of the famous controversy with Elizabeth Anscombe, in response to which Lewis revised his argument.[2] However, in my graduate studies in philosophy I discovered, with some exceptions, that the argument had received little attention even from Christian philosophers and was dismissed by many. As I analyzed the various ways in which the argument could be answered, the firmer the rock appeared on which it stood. And so when it came time to write my doctoral dissertation, I chose to defend this argument against naturalism. Even though my committee was solidly opposed to the conclusion of my argument, they nevertheless passed my dissertation.

I'm still persuaded that Lewis's argument is a good one, and this book is an attempt to show why I think this is so. Before launching into a full-dress discussion of this argument, I think some things need to be said about how Lewis's ideas ought to be adapted in the area of philosophical apologetics.

---

[1]The most developed statement of the argument is found in C. S. Lewis, *Miracles: A Preliminary Study* (New York: Macmillan Paperbacks Edition, 1978), pp. 12-24.
[2]G. E. M. Anscombe, *Metaphysics and the Philosophy of Mind*, vol. 2 of *The Collected Papers of G. E. M. Anscombe* (Minneapolis: University of Minnesota Press, 1981), pp. 224-31.

It seems to me that many discussions of Lewis's arguments treat these arguments as finished products, to be accepted or rejected as they stand. Many treatments of Lewis have been written from a friendly perspective to restate what Lewis has to say for a friendly audience.[3] Others have written about Lewis from a fairly hostile perspective, pointing out, quite correctly, that a skeptical reader will hardly read what Lewis has written and simply change his or her mind.[4] There are, of course, valid points to be made by the side opposing Lewis, but very often the hostile commentator makes these replies as if they were the last word on the subject, relegating Lewis's arguments to the outer darkness of fallacious arguments. Lewis was a thinker with what I believe to be outstanding philosophical instincts. And if he was in error in his thinking, there was usually a little more method in his madness than what would appear to someone who just gives a "refutation" to the error and leaves it at that. And this, I think, is the real test of a great thinker.

But while Lewis's arguments are suggestive, interesting and in my view often sound, he does not answer every question that a critic might ask, nor do we have from him a set of arguments sufficiently polished to persuade persons with technical training in philosophy or other disciplines. And it would be rather surprising if a popular apologist with philosophical training from the 1920s could do this for the benefit of people living in the 1940s, much less the early 2000s.

---

[3]Richard Purtill's *C. S. Lewis's Case for the Christian Faith* (San Francisco: Harper & Row, 1981) is an example of this kind of book.

[4]The only book-length critique of Lewis's apologetics that I know of is John Beversluis's *C. S. Lewis and the Search for Rational Religion* (Grand Rapids, Mich.: Eerdmans, 1985), but there are shorter critiques of Lewis in various publications. Although Beversluis managed to upset many Lewis admirers with his criticisms, he did deal with the substance of Lewis's apologetics, sometimes using biographical material to support his points. Sometimes biographers such as A. N. Wilson and Humphrey Carpenter have offered critical assessments of the substance of Lewis's apologetic arguments with, to my mind, unimpressive results. These biographers frequently engage in ad hominem reasoning, drawing philosophical conclusions not from a real analysis of the relevant arguments, but from biographical hearsay and speculation.

Let me give an example from a philosopher with whom I disagree about nearly everything, David Hume, to help clarify what I am trying to say. It is easy to find mathematical and logical errors in Hume's famous "Of Miracles,"[5] and Lewis is one of those who finds such errors in Hume.[6] But it is not a complete response to Hume to point these out and leave it at that, because Hume raises important issues about the relation of antecedent probability to evidence for miracles that have to be dealt with by anyone who deals seriously with the credibility of miracles. Great thinkers are always the ones that make us think harder for ourselves, not thinkers who do our thinking for us. And the same is true for Lewis. If you think Lewis is mistaken, I believe that Lewis is a sufficiently great thinker that one must do more than point out errors on the surface. One must dig deeper, see how Lewis's thought might be developed, and try to show that no good arguments are forthcoming along those lines.

Perhaps Lewis's most famous argument is what is known as the Lewis trilemma. It is unreasonable, Lewis says, to say that Christ was a great moral teacher but not God, because he claimed, both implicitly and explicitly, to be God. If he wasn't God, he either had to be lying, which would make him wicked, or he had to be deluded, which would make him insane. Since these two alternatives are implausible, Lewis says that he must be telling the truth and really be God.[7]

Many others have repeated this argument in their own apologetics.[8] The argument makes four assumptions, however, and critics of the argument have challenged all these assumptions.

---

[5]David Hume, *Enquiry Concerning Human Understanding*, ed. L. A. Selby-Bigge (1902; reprint, Oxford: Oxford University Press, 1972), see essay 10, "Of Miracles," pp. 109-31.
[6]Lewis, *Miracles*, chap. 13, "On Probability," pp. 100-107.
[7]C. S. Lewis, *Mere Christianity* (New York: Macmillan Paperbacks Edition, 1960), pp. 54-56.
[8]Notably Josh McDowell, *Evidence That Demands a Verdict* (Arrowhead Springs, Calif.: Campus Crusade for Christ International, 1972). Andrew Rilstone, objecting strongly to McDowell's appropriation of the argument, argues that the trilemma argument was intended as a wake-up call for those who take the claims of Christ too lightly and not as hard

1. Jesus' claims in Scripture are best interpreted not merely as claims to be the Jews' Messiah but as claims to be God.

2. The Gospels are a reliable historical record of what Jesus said and did.

3. No sane person can form the false belief that he himself is God.

4. The claim "Jesus is God" is more antecedently probable than the admittedly improbable claim that Jesus was a great moral teacher and either a liar or a madman.

Lewis supplies some argumentation in defense of all of these claims in various parts of his writings, and it seems to me that there is a good deal to be said on both sides of each of these claims before a full assessment can be reached. If all these assumptions are defensible, then the argument is a good one. But rather than debating these assumptions, apologists have simply repeated the mantra "liar, lunatic or Lord," while opponents have cried in response "false dilemma." Neither of these responses, in my estimation, does justice to the complex issues the trilemma raises.

The trilemma, unfortunately, is not the subject I wish to discuss in this book; I mention it merely to show how Lewis can either be offered as a final answer or be offered as a spur to think the relevant issues through oneself. The way one honors Lewis's apologetic achievement, it seems to me, is not simply by repeating what he says, but by developing his ideas, asking probing questions of them and developing the discussion in ways that reflect one's own thinking as well as Lewis's. The result of such reflection on my part has persuaded me that, indeed, Christianity is credible for approximately the reasons that Lewis said it was. I believe that, to a large extent, not enough of this further reflection is present in the secondary Lewis lit-

---

proof that Christianity is true ("Fool, Charlatan or Evangelist? C. S. Lewis, Josh McDowell and the 'Trilemma,'" The Life and Opinions of Andrew Rilstone, Gentleman, <http://www.aslan.demon.co.uk/trilemma.htm>).

erature, and that is why I believe that despite Lewis's enormous popularity, subsequent apologists have underutilized the resources that he has provided for them.

Besides the tendency to let C. S. Lewis think for us, I must mention that another obstacle to the serious consideration of Lewis's arguments is just plain snobbery. I once presented a paper on the ex-change between Lewis and Elizabeth Anscombe at a secular philosophy department where I was a visiting instructor. In that paper I argued (as I shall argue later in this book) that Lewis's argument against naturalism could surmount the challenges that Anscombe posed for it. Most of the faculty there told me that I had not persuaded them that Lewis's argument was a good one, but I had shown that Lewis had adequate responses available to him to meet Anscombe's challenge. One older professor of known positivist tendencies told me that I had written a good paper on reasons and causes, but the main problem with it was that I had chosen a "patsy" (Lewis) to devote my energies to. Never mind that I had (apparently) successfully defended Lewis against Anscombe, he was still a patsy and not worthy of serious discussion. It is sometimes presupposed by those who are familiar with the technical side of a discipline like philosophy that no one who is not similarly a "professional" has anything serious to say. But of course "professionalism" in philosophy is a rather recent development: the majority of those who have made significant contributions to philosophy over the past twenty-five centuries would not qualify as "professional" philosophers in the contemporary sense.

C. S. LEWIS AND THE "ANSCOMBE LEGEND"
A further factor inhibiting serious discussion of Lewis is that his career as an apologist is often assessed biographically, focusing on Lewis himself rather than what he had to say. So, for example, it is often suggested that Lewis was profoundly upset by his exchange

with Anscombe, and therefore he himself realized his apologetic arguments were inadequate. Analysts often arrive at this conclusion without considering the points at issue in the debate. Thus a kind of "Anscombe legend" has shrouded Lewis's apologetic career, which in many minds seems to have outlived the actual arguments Lewis and Anscombe presented.[9] The following passage, from Humphrey Carpenter's *The Inklings*, is a case in point:

> *Miracles* was published in 1947. Early the following year, its third chapter, in which Lewis proved that human Reason is independent of the natural world, was publicly attacked at the Socratic Club, not by an atheist, but by a fellow Christian, the Catholic philosopher Elizabeth Anscombe. Lewis was unprepared for the severely critical analysis to which she submitted his arguments, for she proved in her turn that his "proof" was severely faulty. It is true that Lewis's most fervent supporters felt that she had not demonstrated her point successfully, but many who were at the meeting thought that a conclusive blow had been struck against one of his most fundamental arguments. Certainly after it was all over Lewis himself was in very low spirits. . . .
>
> Lewis had learnt his lesson: for after this he wrote no further books of Christian apologetics for ten years, apart from a collection of sermons; and when he did publish another apologetic work, *Reflections on the Psalms*, it was notably quieter in tone and did not attempt any further intellectual proofs of theism or Christianity. Though he continued to believe in the importance of Reason in relation to his Christian faith, he had perhaps realized the truth of Charles Williams' maxim, "No one can possibly do more than decide what to believe."[10]

---

[9]My use of the term "Anscombe legend" is based on a comment by J. R. Lucas, who wrote, "The received version should be treated with some caution: Professor Mitchell, who attended all the meetings of the Socratic Club at that time, has no memory of the encounter. Oxford legends often owe more to the attitudes of those who report them than to the facts which allegedly they report" (J. R. Lucas, "The Restoration of Man: A Lecture Given in Durham on Thursday, October 22, 1992," J. R. Lucas Home Page, <http://users .ox.ac.uk/~jlucas/lewis.html>).

[10]Humphrey Carpenter, *The Inklings* (London: Allen & Unwin, 1978), pp. 238-39.

Now it is important to see what is missing in this discussion: any treatment of what the arguments of Lewis and Anscombe actually were. Apparently Carpenter thinks he can draw the conclusion that Anscombe had shown Lewis's argument to be "severely faulty" without analyzing the arguments themselves, simply based on biographical considerations. Nor is it indicated here that Lewis revised the argument in the 1960 Fontana edition to meet Anscombe's objections. In A. N. Wilson's biography, the Anscombe legend is pushed to extreme lengths: the incident's psychological impact explains Lewis's "retreat" into children's fantasy (Narnia), the fact that a female witch offers skeptical arguments in *The Silver Chair* that nearly beguile the protagonists of that story, and the fact that Lewis enjoyed corresponding with American women (including Joy Davidman).[11]

John Beversluis, in his book *C. S. Lewis and the Search for Rational Religion* and in his essay for *Christian History* entitled "Beyond the Double-Bolted Door,"[12] also makes a good deal of the psychological impact of the Anscombe incident and so uses the Anscombe legend to support his claim that Lewis's apologetics are woefully inadequate from a philosophical perspective. But he also argues in favor of the claim that "the arguments that Anscombe presented can be pressed further, and Lewis's revised argument does nothing to meet them,"[13] and he does analyze the actual arguments. Very much to his credit, however, in his subsequent review of Wilson's book, he abandons the Anscombe legend entirely:

> First, the Anscombe debate was by no means Lewis's first exposure to a professional philosopher: he lived among them all his adult life, read the Greats, and even taught philosophy. Second, it is simply un-

---

[11]A. N. Wilson, *C. S. Lewis: A Biography* (New York: W. W. Norton, 1990).
[12]John Beversluis, "Beyond the Double-Bolted Door," *Christian History* 4, no. 3 (1985): 28-31.
[13]Beversluis, *C. S. Lewis and the Search*, p. 73.

true that the post-Anscombe Lewis abandoned Christian apologetics. In 1960 he published a second edition of *Miracles* in which he revised the third chapter and thereby replied to Anscombe. Third, most printed discussions of the debate, mine included, fail to mention that Anscombe herself complimented Lewis's revised argument on the grounds that it is deeper and far more serious than the original version. Finally, the myth that Lewis abandoned Christian apologetics overlooks several post-Anscombe articles, among them "Is Theism Important?" (1952)—a discussion of Christianity and theism which touches on philosophical proofs for God's existence—and "On Obstinacy of Belief"—in which Lewis defends the rationality of belief in God in the face of apparently contrary evidence (*the* issue in philosophical theology during the late 1950s and early 60s). It is rhetorically effective to announce that the post-Anscombe Lewis wrote no further books on Christian apologetics, but it is pure fiction. Even if it were true, what would this Argument from Abandoned Subjects prove? He wrote no further books on *Paradise Lost* or courtly love either.[14]

Anscombe herself does not recall any devastating encounter and attributes the adverse reaction of some of Lewis's friends in terms of the phenomenon of projection.[15] Anyone who has presented papers at philosophy conferences knows that the process of criticism and revision is just how things get done in that discipline. At such meetings, typically a presenter presents a paper, and a commentator offers a critical response. Sometimes the critical response is completely devastating to the arguments of the presenter. But more frequently the commentator finds difficulties with the paper that force the presenter to revise and strengthen his arguments. And this seems to have been exactly what happened in the Lewis-Anscombe controversy.

---

[14]John Beversluis, "Surprised by Freud: A Critical Appraisal of A. N. Wilson's Biography of C. S. Lewis," *Christianity and Literature* 41, no. 2 (1992): 179-95.
[15]Anscombe, *Metaphysics*, p. 10.

DID LEWIS DROP OUT OF THE GAME?

I do believe that Lewis, partly as a result of the Anscombe incident, came to feel ill-equipped to deal with the philosophy of his day. But this need not be looked on as a confession of general philosophical incompetence. Part of the job of a professional philosopher is to be responsive to the major philosophical movements of one's time. When Lewis received his philosophical training, the philosophy of absolute idealism was a major player in the philosophical debate, and anyone who wanted to do philosophy in that time would have to come to terms with absolute idealism. In a philosophy department today one can go through an entire Ph.D. program without ever having to come to terms with absolute idealism, except as part of a historical survey of nineteenth- or early twentieth-century philosophy. In the 1920s, if one had something to say about language, for example, that was opposed to the philosophy of absolute idealism, one would have to respond to what the idealists would say. Now, of course, the absolute idealist response can safely be ignored.

In the 1940s and 1950s in Oxford, logical positivism was the big item on the philosophical map. According to the positivist verification principle, a statement about the world is meaningful only in the case that it can be empirically verified. Using this principle, A. J. Ayer, in *Language, Truth and Logic*, declared theology and metaphysics meaningless in just a couple of pages.[16] And many religious philosophers became very worried that their statements failed this criterion of meaning and would have to be abandoned as nonsense, often offering reductionist analyses of religious language that abandoned the straightforward truth claims of historic Christianity. But in philosophy the tide has turned against these types of objections to the meaningfulness of religious language, so much so that when the atheist philosopher Kai Nielsen attempted to argue that theism was

---

[16]A. J. Ayer, *Language, Truth and Logic* (Harmondsworth: Penguin, 1990), pp. 119-21.

meaningless in his 1988 debate with Christian philosopher J. P. Moreland, it was agreed by most commentators on the debate, including
atheists, that this strategy was a signal failure. In fact, the president of
the Internet Infidels, the leading atheist site on the World Wide Web,
refused to recommend purchasing the book from that debate to his
fellow atheists because he thinks that Nielsen's strategy was badly
misguided and resulted in a decisive victory for Moreland![17]

Now if you are a professional philosopher, you have to write for philosophy journals, and whether you like it or not your work has to be responsive to the main philosophical developments of your day, because
that is what your referees will have been reading. So Lewis did not develop a detailed response to logical positivism, or to Witt-genstein's
philosophy, or to other current developments, and so one could say
with Austin Farrer that he "dropped out of the game."[18] One could, it
seems to me, develop a response to those movements based on elements of Lewis's thought, but Lewis did not do this, and so he can't be
regarded as a "real philosopher" in at least one sense. But as our century turns, we have little need to ask how we can respond to positivist
objections to Christian theism, any more than we need to know how
to answer an absolute idealist. We do need to address the problems of
philosophical naturalism or materialism, and with respect to these issues Lewis provides us with some important arguments.

A comprehensive materialism, while itself a position inimical to
Christian theism, is nonetheless, like Christian theism, an attempt to
generate a synoptic worldview and is not simply a matter of analyzing
language. Such materialism would have to be rejected as nonsense
by a strict interpretation of logical positivism. J. J. C. Smart, in his

---

[17]The Moreland-Nielsen debate was published in *Does God Exist?* (Amherst, N.Y.:
Prometheus, 1993). The response by Jeffrey Lowder, former president of Internet Infidels,
is found at The Secular Web feedback page <www.infidels.org/infidels/feedback/1998/
january.html>.
[18]Austin Farrer, "The Christian Apologist," in *Light on C. S. Lewis*, ed. Jocelyn Gibb (London: Geoffrey Bles, 1965), p. 40.

book *Philosophy and Scientific Realism*, attempted to bring philosophy back to the effort to provide a synoptic worldview based on science, and philosophers since have acknowledged that worldview development is an important role for philosophy.[19]

Although the secular philosophical community often sets the agenda for how philosophy will be done, in the last couple of decades Christian philosophers have taken matters into their own hands. Alvin Plantinga, in one of the earliest issues of the journal *Faith and Philosophy*, urged Christian philosophers to look at things from their own Christian perspective rather than carving out areas of thought where God-talk would be acceptable to nonbelievers.[20] What follows from this is that if Christians get an idea from Lewis, they need not wait for Lewis to become respectable to the philosophical community at large before exploring his ideas and arguments.

DID C. S. LEWIS LOSE HIS APOLOGETICS IN *A GRIEF OBSERVED*?

The screenplay, play and film *Shadowlands* paint a picture of a Lewis who abandons his Christian confidence in the face of the tragedy of his wife's death, maintaining his religious beliefs only through a leap of faith. Quite coincidentally, Beversluis, whose book came out about the same time as the screenplay, maintains that Lewis abandoned his apologetic stance in the course of his grief experience, and that to retain his faith he defended it on grounds completely alien to the grounds he had used in his other apologetic writings. In particular, Beversluis maintains that in the course of *A Grief Observed*, Lewis implicitly shifts from a Platonist to an Ockhamist conception of God and

---

[19]J. J. C. Smart, *Philosophy and Scientific Realism* (London: Routledge & Kegan Paul, 1960), chap. 1.
[20]Alvin Plantinga, "Advice to Christian Philosophers," *Faith and Philosophy* 1, no. 3 (1984): 253-71; it also appears online with a new preface at <http://www.leaderu.com/truth/1truth10/html>.

thereby embraces a fideistic understanding of faith and reason, jettisoning his entire previous apologetic work. *Platonism* is defined by Beversluis as the view that God's goodness is to be understood in a way that is continuous with our normal conceptions of goodness. Lewis had previously argued that the conception of God as good made sense only if that concept of goodness was continuous with our own. But Beversluis maintains that in the course of his grief experience, Lewis accepted a view of God according to which God's actions are right just because it is God who performs them.[21] With this latter view, which Beversluis calls Ockhamism, no one can complain if God, before the foundation of the world, chose a few people to be saved and all the rest to be punished everlastingly. That this is an affront to human reason, according to Ockhamism, only shows that (natural) human reason is fallen and part of our desperately wicked human nature. Indeed, it is not surprising to discover that Ockhamism is popular amongst Calvinists, including Calvin himself.

But a careful reading of *A Grief Observed* suggests that Lewis not only did not abandon his previous apologetic arguments, but in fact reaffirms his arguments, including his arguments against Ockhamism. Lewis in his youth had been an atheist who rejected theism based on the argument from evil, and he had even written poetry from that perspective.[22] Echoing that earlier atheistic perspective, Lewis speaks of God in the early part of *A Grief Observed* as "a very absent help in trouble," a "Cosmic Sadist" and an "Eternal Vivisector."[23]

But it seems evident to me that Lewis's primary reasons for coming to accept the good God of Christianity were not that he thought he had some overwhelmingly plausible explanation for all the evils in the world, but rather that alternative worldviews had even more se-

---

[21]Beversluis, *C. S. Lewis and the Search*, pp. 102-3.
[22]C. S. Lewis, *Spirits in Bondage: A Cycle of Lyrics* (San Diego: Harcourt Brace Jovanovich, 1984).
[23]C. S. Lewis, *A Grief Observed* (New York: Bantam, 1976), esp. pp. 5, 35.

rious difficulties with them, and his treatment of these issues in *A Grief Observed* reflects this outlook on the problem. In *A Grief Observed*, Lewis briefly considers three possible alternatives to belief in a God whose goodness is commensurate with the way in which we use the concept of goodness in our ordinary discourse about humans: naturalistic atheism, the cosmic sadist hypothesis and Ockhamism. All of these alternatives, however, are rejected in the course of *A Grief Observed* for much the same reasons that they are rejected in his apologetic writings. It is true that the book is primarily pastoral, addressed to the grieving believer (first and foremost Lewis himself) rather than to the skeptic. Nevertheless the book does contain some argumentation to show that his grief experience does not provide any reason to adopt a worldview other than theism that includes a Platonistic conception of divine goodness.

Let us consider the situation with respect to naturalism or materialism. In his apologetics Lewis had criticized naturalism because he considered it inconsistent with the validity of reasoning. One aspect of the argument from reason is the idea that physical states cannot be true or false. It is presented in the essay "De Futilitate":

> We are compelled to admit between the thoughts of a terrestrial astronomer and the behavior of matter several light-years away that particular relation we call truth. But this relation has no meaning at all if we try to make it exist between the matter of the star and the astronomer's brain, considered as a lump of matter. The brain may be in all sorts of relations to the star no doubt: it is in a spatial relation, and a time relation, and a quantitative relation. But to talk of one bit of matter being true of another seems to be nonsense. It might turn out to be the case that every atom in the universe thought, and thought truly, about every other. But that relation between any two atoms would be something quite distinct from the physical relations between them.[24]

---

[24]C. S. Lewis, "De Futilitate," in *Christian Reflections* (Grand Rapids, Mich.: Eerdmans, 1967), pp. 63-64.

In *A Grief Observed*, in explaining why in the face of his wife's death Lewis does not believe she has ceased to exist, he echoes this argument, though he talks in terms of falsity rather than truth:

> If H [Joy] "is not" then she never was. I mistook a cloud of atoms for a person. There aren't and never were, any people. Death only reveals the vacuity that was always there. What we call the living are simply those who have not yet been unmasked. All equally bankrupt, but some not yet declared. But this must be nonsense; vacuity revealed to whom? bankruptcy declared to whom? To other boxes of fireworks or clouds of atoms. I will never believe—more strictly I can't believe— that one set of physical events could be, or make, a mistake about other sets.[25]

In other words, Lewis considered materialism just as self-refuting as he always had. The argument he presents is hardly designed to persuade a skeptical philosopher like Anscombe or Beversluis, but it is a reaffirmation of his previous arguments.

Another counterposition he considers is the possibility that God is not a good being but a cosmic sadist, and he finds this idea also unacceptable. Beversluis explains this by saying that "the shift [from Platonism to Ockhamism] occurs when Lewis begins to suspect that the hypothesis of the Cosmic Sadist is too anthropomorphic. According to such a view, God is like the man who tortures his cats, and that is unbearable."[26] But for Lewis, such a view of God is not simply unbearable; it is nonsensical. In *Mere Christianity* Lewis had considered the view he called dualism, according to which there is a good being and an evil being, both coeternal, who struggle for the control of the universe. Although Lewis finds this to be, "next to Christianity, the manliest and most sensible creed on the market," he finds it open to serious criticisms. These criticisms are precisely the criticisms he

---

[25]Lewis, *A Grief Observed*, pp. 8-9.
[26]Beversluis, *C. S. Lewis and the Search*, p. 150.

levels at the hypothesis of the cosmic sadist in *A Grief Observed*. Consider the following passage from *Mere Christianity*:

> If Dualism is true, then the bad Power must be a being who likes badness for its own sake. But in reality we have no experience of anyone liking badness just because it is bad. The nearest we can get to it is in cruelty. But in real life people are cruel because they have a sexual perversion, which makes cruelty cause a sensual pleasure in them, or else for the sake of something they are going to get out of it—money, or power, or safety. But pleasure, money, power, and safety are all, as far as they go, good things. The badness consists in pursuing them by the wrong method, or in the wrong way, or too much. I do not mean, of course, that the people who do this are not desperately wicked. I do mean that wickedness, when you examine it, turns out to be the pursuit of some good in the wrong way. You can be good for the mere sake of goodness, you cannot be bad for the mere sake of badness. . . . In other words badness cannot succeed even in being bad in the same way in which goodness is good. Goodness is, so to speak, itself: badness is only spoiled goodness. And there must be something good first before it can be spoiled.[27]

A moment's reflection will reveal that this is not only an argument against dualism, but also against the doctrine of the cosmic sadist. The idea that the creator of the universe might be evil is not plausible since evil cannot exist on its own, but is always a perversion of good. And this apologetic argument is what Lewis uses to respond to the thesis of the cosmic sadist in *A Grief Observed*.

> But the picture I was building up last night is simply the picture of a man like S.C.—who used to sit next to me at dinner and tell me what he'd been doing to the cats that afternoon. Now a being like S.C., however, glorified, couldn't invent or create or govern anything. He would set traps and try to bait them. But he'd never have

---

[27]Lewis, *Mere Christianity*, p. 49.

thought of baits like love, or laughter, or daffodils, or a frosty sunset. *He* make a universe? He couldn't make a joke, or a bow, or an apology, or a friend.[28]

Finally, and most critically, Lewis considers the possibility of replacing his good-in-our-sense God hypothesis with Ockhamism, the view that God's sadistic conduct is in the final analysis justified because we are so fallen and depraved that our ideas of goodness simply do not count. According to Ockhamism, actions and commands are right because God does them; according to Platonism, God does what God does because it is right. If God were to announce a new, reversed set of Ten Commandments, which commanded adultery, homicide and theft, an Ockhamist would say that these actions would be right because they were divinely commanded. In previous writings Lewis had harshly criticized Ockhamism. In *The Problem of Pain* he wrote:

> It has sometimes been asked whether God commands certain things because they are right, or whether certain things are right because God commands them. With Hooker, and against Dr. Johnson, I emphatically embrace the first alternative. The second might lead to the abominable conclusion (reached, I think, by Paley) that charity is good only because God arbitrarily commanded it—that He might equally well have commanded us to hate Him and one another and that hatred would then have been right. I believe, on the contrary, that "they err who think that of the will of God to do this or that there is no reason besides his will."[29]

Beversluis maintains that Lewis accepts Ockhamism in *A Grief Observed*. But actually, that is the very book in which Lewis presents

---

[28] Lewis, *A Grief Observed*, pp. 139-61. The claim of this passage in *A Grief Observed* is precisely the same as the point made in the *Mere Christianity* passage: neither a wicked man like S. C. nor Satan could create anything; they can only pervert things that have already been created good.

[29] C. S. Lewis, *The Problem of Pain* (New York: Macmillan Paperbacks Edition, 1962), p. 100.

his most penetrating critique of Ockhamism. In most of his writings, Lewis is content to point out the morally disastrous consequences of Ockhamism. In *A Grief Observed*, Lewis points out that Ockhamism has disastrous consequences for knowledge as well:

> And so what? This, for all practical (and speculative) purposes sponges God off the slate. The word *good*, as applied to him, becomes meaningless: like abracadabra. We have no motive for obeying Him. Not even fear. It is true that we have His threats and promises. But why should we believe them? If cruelty is from His point of view "good," telling lies may be "good" too. Even if they are true, what then? If His ideas of good are so very different from ours, what He calls "Heaven" might well be what we should call Hell, and vice versa. Finally, if reality at its very root is so meaningless to us—or, putting it the other way round, if we are such total imbeciles—what is the point of trying to think either about God or about anything else? The knot comes undone when you try to pull it tight.[30]

René Descartes, in order to raise skeptical doubts about even our firmest certainties, imagined that we might be under the influence of an evil demon, and more modern philosophers have speculated about the possibility of our being brains in vats. The Ockhamist hypothesis (and surely the cosmic sadist hypothesis as well) is as epistemically damaging as the brain in the vat hypothesis. Under these hypotheses we will believe the truth only if a powerful being whose motives are either wicked or incomprehensible chooses that we should believe the truth, and not otherwise. These theses are, in Lewis's view, equally as self-refuting as is naturalism. If they are true then no one could know this or anything else.

Of course, the above discussion does not demonstrate that these arguments are good ones, but only that Lewis continued to employ them throughout his career, even in the face of personal tragedy. I

---

[30]Lewis, *A Grief Observed*, pp. 37-38.

have been at some pains to show the continuity between Lewis's apologetic writings and A *Grief Observed*, a continuity that, so far as I can tell, has gone unnoticed by many commentators and been denied outright by others. It is true that Lewis experienced a dark night of doubt and came to believe that his faith had been unreal. But what does that mean? It is my contention that it had absolutely nothing to do with the grounds of his intellectual assent to Christian theism. Rather, faith in this context should be understood as trust. The intellectual foundations of his faith were not shaken by his grief experience, as he reminded himself during the writing of the notebooks that became A *Grief Observed*. Nevertheless he experienced doubt. After reaching the conclusion that he had no real new grounds for abandoning his faith in favor of any counterposition, he still had to deal with his loss and understand why these doubts had arisen. And in doing so he concluded that he did not have the firm trust in God's wisdom that he had thought he had. But while this is a serious admission, it says nothing about the apologetic grounds on which he assented intellectually. The message of A *Grief Observed* is that those intellectual grounds remained what they had always been.

I think it is time for us to examine Lewis's thought fairly and honestly, not expecting either inerrancy or rank amateurism, but rather an incisive and powerful mind with many ideas that need to be pursued further. Moreover, we should resist, as much as possible, the "personal heresy" of focusing on Lewis himself rather than what he had to say.

Assessing Apologetic Arguments

THIS BOOK IS PRIMARILY CONCERNED with an apologetic argument or, as we shall see, a set of apologetic arguments against naturalism and for some kind of religious worldview. But what constitutes a successful apologetic argument? This is an important issue; often arguments in defense of religious belief are considered abject failures because they fail to meet standards that almost no philosophical argument ever meets. In answering this question, philosophers of religion have done a great deal to provide a helpful understanding of an argument's success.

To develop this discussion of how we are to evaluate arguments in apologetics, a widely used text in philosophy of religion will be helpful. *Reason and Religious Belief*, by Peterson, Hasker, Reichenbach and Basinger, distinguishes three positions in the relation between faith and reason: fideism, strong rationalism and critical rationalism.[1]

FIDEISM

Fideism is the view that religious beliefs are not open to rational evaluation. The fundamental convictions of the Christian belief must simply be accepted without question. The attitude of fideism was neatly summed in a comment I once heard Jimmy Swaggart make: "Man can't use his mind to know the truth; if he uses his mind he just comes up with something stupid like the theory of evolution."

In the fideist view, of course, employing a philosophical argument

---

[1]Michael Peterson, William Hasker, Bruce Reichenbach and David Basinger, *Reason and Religious Belief* (New York: Oxford University Press, 1990).

like Lewis's argument against naturalism is inappropriate. The basic beliefs of one's religious faith system are not open to question. As will be seen in chapter six, religious believers are not the only fideists. Philosophical naturalists sometimes have made fideistic assertions, removing their own basic position from the possibility of rational assessment.

C. S. Lewis is generally not thought of as a fideist, although Beversluis maintains that Lewis adopted a fideist response to the problem of evil in A *Grief Observed*.[2] But I believe I have refuted the claim that A *Grief Observed* reflects a fundamental shift in Lewis's apologetic stance, so this contention can be set aside here. In any event, Lewis employs philosophical arguments in *Miracles*, and clearly Lewis did not intend for these arguments to be dismissed on fideistic grounds.

But fideism is difficult to maintain consistently. Consider how even Jimmy Swaggart would respond to someone who, instead of accepting Christianity, believed himself to be created in the image of superheroes whose deeds are recorded in the sacred Marvel Comics.[3] He might respond by suggesting the rational implausibility of such a belief, but from the point of view of fideism, he is not supposed to engage in this kind of rational evaluation. After all, man can't use his mind to know the truth. On the other hand, suggesting that Marvelism conflicts with the Bible will hardly cut any ice with someone who accepts a different set of holy books. While some religious believers (and nonbelievers) want to shield some of their beliefs from rational assessment, it is very difficult to shield them all.

STRONG RATIONALISM

If we insist that religious beliefs be open to rational assessment, how should we assess the evidence? When Lewis's arguments are evaluated,

---

[2]John Beversluis, *C. S. Lewis and the Search for Rational Religion* (Grand Rapids, Mich.: Eerdmans, 1985), pp. 140-61.
[3]This example was used by atheist Douglas Jesseph during the question and answer session of a debate with William Lane Craig held at Arizona State University in 1997.

they are often evaluated as attempts to fulfill the requirements of a doctrine that the textbook authors call strong rationalism. Strong rationalism is the view that in order for a religious belief system to be properly and rationally accepted, it must be possible to prove that the belief system is true. But what is it to prove that a position is true? As understood by strong rationalists, the word *prove* means to show that a belief is true in a way that *should* be convincing to any reasonable person.

Now clearly no arguments about, say, belief in the existence of God are satisfying to everyone. There are atheists and theists at the highest levels of education. But the strong rationalist can maintain that while the case for belief (or unbelief) is not *in fact* convincing to everyone, it *should* be. The evidence is strong enough to convince everyone who is well informed and rational; if a well-informed person rejects the evidence; it is rejected because he suffers from some species of cognitive pathology—that is, some kind of failure or inability to recognize the truth.[4] Consider what many academics believe about astrology. Surely there are plenty of people who believe in astrology, but I at least am inclined to suppose that a careful study of astrological beliefs will show that it is not reasonable to accept these claims.

Bertrand Russell, for example, thought the case against believing in God was so strong that he was prepared to explain anyone's belief in God's existence in terms of three fears: the fear of death, the fear of hell and the fear that the universe should be meaningless. In his essay "The Value of Free Thought," Russell defined free thought not in terms of rejection of traditional religious beliefs, but in terms of how beliefs are formed.[5] A freethinker's belief formation processes,

---

[4]By "cognitive pathology" I do not mean to suggest that people who fall prey to these failures of reason are in need of attention from mental health professionals. But these processes are inimical to the healthy state of a cognitive life, namely, the knowledge of the truth.

[5]Bertrand Russell, "The Value of Free Thought," in *Understanding History* (New York: Philosophical Library, 1957), pp. 57-58. For a detailed discussion on whether Christians can ever be regarded as freethinkers see Jeffrey Lowder, "Is Free-Thinker Synonymous

he maintained, are free from the force of tradition and the tyranny of one's passions. By this definition a Christian could be a freethinker. One might be inclined to suppose that someone like C. S. Lewis, who by his own account was brought "kicking and screaming" into Christianity in spite of his emotional disposition to reject it, would qualify as a freethinker. But it is very clear from reading Russell's essay that while Russell is willing to countenance the *possibility* of there being a Christian who satisfies the definition of a freethinker, he holds that the class of *actual* Christian freethinkers is empty. Consider these comments about his involvement in the process of selecting a philosopher at a major university:

> I was myself at one time officially concerned in the appointment of a philosophy professor at an important American university; all the others agreed that of course he must be a good Christian. Practically all philosophers of any intellectual eminence are openly or secretly freethinkers; the insistence on orthodoxy therefore necessitated the appointment of a nonentity or a humbug.[6]

Apparently Russell ruled out the possibility of hiring a Christian freethinker, although he allowed for the possibility in his definition of free thought.

I don't know what Russell would have said to Lewis's claim that he came to believe in spite of his wishes to the contrary, but I suppose that he would very likely not have accepted his autobiographical claims on face value. Since Russell firmly believed all rational defenses of theism to be so weak that anyone with any intelligence should be able to see through them, the only explanation for the existence of someone like Lewis is that he was involved in some kind of self-deception. According to people like Russell, Lewis thought he was accepting theism and

with Non-Theist," The Secular Web, Modern Library (updated October 13, 2001) <www.infidels.org/library/modern/features/2000/lowder1/html>.
[6] Russell, "Value of Free Thought," p. 94.

Christianity because they were supported by rational arguments, but in fact these rational arguments are rationalizations for beliefs chosen for preintellectual reasons. On this account, we should perhaps not be too surprised by the decidedly Freudian perspective we find in some well-known accounts of Lewis's life, notably A. N. Wilson's.[7]

But nonbelievers are not the only people who make strong rationalist claims on behalf of their own beliefs and explain their opponents' beliefs in terms of cognitive pathology. In his widely read *Evidence That Demands a Verdict*, the Christian apologist Josh McDowell says that the case for the resurrection of Jesus and the claims of Christianity are so powerful that "the rejection of Christ is usually not so much of the 'mind' as of the will, not so much 'I can't' but 'I won't.'"[8] McDowell's account of cognitive pathology, like Russell's, is threefold. Most students reject Christ because of ignorance, usually self-imposed(!), pride or a moral problem. People do not want to accept a Lord over their life; they do not want to have to admit that they are sinners; they do not want there to be a God who has the right, power and authority to give commandments; they may be engaged in behavior that is regarded by Christians as sinful, and so they are motivated to find any excuse they can to remain unbelievers.

Now you might notice that it is pretty easy to come up with these sorts of explanations for our opponents' beliefs; in fact it is a little too easy. What is difficult is to come up with a case in favor of one's own beliefs that is sufficiently strong to warrant the strong rationalist's claims on behalf of his or her own position, either theistic or atheistic. Despite Russell's and McDowell's bombastic claims concerning the state of the evidence for and against the claims of theism and Christianity, I doubt that there are many careful students of the arguments on both sides who would say that the case pre-

---

[7]A. N. Wilson, *C. S. Lewis: A Biography* (New York: W. W. Norton, 1990).
[8]Josh McDowell, *Evidence that Demands a Verdict* (Arrowhead Springs, Calif.: Campus Crusade for Christ International, 1972).

sented by either of these men supports the kind of strong claims that each is inclined to make. Russell, for example, grossly misrepresents theistic arguments such as Thomas Aquinas's cosmological argument.[9] McDowell hardly presents a balanced statement of the evidence, quoting almost exclusively from sources friendly to his own conclusions.[10]

The claim that one side or the other in some highly controversial issue such as theism has a monopoly on rationality is thought by most philosophers to be an extremely difficult claim to defend. This sort of claim would be easier to defend if there were certain beliefs that serve for all persons as appropriate starting points, for then we could figure out whether or not, say, the belief in the existence of God could be derived from those claims. Then we could say to people, "Empty yourself of all your philosophical predispositions, start with only those beliefs that can be set upon a secure foundation, and reason from there." Then, if two people come to different conclusions, we can go back to the beginning and see where the error might have been committed. In mathematics, if two people reach two different conclusions, we can retrace their steps to see where their thinking diverged to see which one has committed an error.

But what is supposed to constitute such a philosophical foundation? Descartes began his philosophizing by rejecting every proposition that could possibly be doubted, including his beliefs in the external world, in hopes of finding some beliefs about which he could be absolutely certain and on which he could build his belief

---

[9]In "Why I Am Not a Christian" Russell presents the cosmological argument as if it were committed to the claim that everything has a cause (in which case God would have to have one, and we would have no logical stopping place) when a more reasonable version of the cosmological argument would be that everything that contingently exists has a cause of its existence. That version of the causal principle would not require that God have a cause, since ex hypothesi God exists necessarily (in "Thinkers on Religion," [2002] <http://jeromekahn123.tripod.com/thinkersonreligion/id7.html>).

[10]For a critique of McDowell see Jeffrey Lowder, ed., "The Jury Is In: The Ruling on McDowell's 'Evidence,'" The Secular Web, Modern Library (2000) <www.infidels.org /library/modern/jeff_lowder/jury/index.shtml>.

system. There is pretty much a consensus in philosophy that Descartes's project was a manifest failure and, what is more, attempts to revise the project by, say, starting from experience as opposed to reason were equally unsuccessful.

What seems impossible to achieve is a neutral perspective from which to evaluate controversial philosophical claims. Everyone comes to inquiry with experiences, background beliefs and other intellectual predispositions. It's not too surprising that people whose experiences in Christian churches are pleasant are more inclined to find the claims of Christianity plausible than those whose experiences in Christian churches are unpleasant. Are differences at even the highest levels of education grounds for supposing that even some of the smartest people just won't listen to reason, or is it rather evidence that there are different perspectives from which inquiry proceeds?

Consider, for example, evidence for the resurrection of Jesus. Some people find the evidence for Jesus' resurrection to be quite sufficient to support this crucial doctrine of the Christian faith. Others find the evidence very flimsy. Should this disagreement be explained simply in terms of cognitive pathology on one side? I doubt it. But what I am inclined to suppose is that while for some people Jesus' resurrection is in accordance with their background beliefs (they believe that God exists, they believe that God is likely to have manifested his presence somewhere in the world, etc.), others do not believe that any being exists capable of causing Jesus to rise from his grave. Obviously this will affect how much evidence is going to be required to accept the resurrection. Lewis's book *Miracles* clearly shows an awareness of this; he considers it useless to try to show that the central miracles of Christianity are true without providing some reasons why these miracle claims should not be dismissed out of hand as either impossible (because naturalism or some other worldview that is not miracle-tolerant is true) or because it is maximally improbable (the conclusion of Hume's probabilistic argument against miracle claims).[11]

While it is an error to use cognitive pathology to account for the fact that one's opponents take the positions that they take, I think that cognitive pathology can show us how difficult it is to establish the rationality of controversial beliefs about claims as critical as theism. When Bertrand Russell tells me that if I believe in God, I only believe because I am afraid of hell, afraid of extinction or afraid that the universe should be meaningless, I have to admit that I do find fears of that sort within my own mind. What I find objectionable in Russell is his utter unwillingness to consider the fact that all the nonrational motives do not lie on the side of the believer and this discounting of all rational motivations on the part of the believer. McDowell is surely right in pointing out the nonrational motives of unbelievers, although he makes the same mistake Russell does in assuming that his side is somehow free of nonrational motivations and failing to recognize rational motivations on the part of nonbelievers. My point here is that while it is important to be as rational as possible concerning religious beliefs, one should recognize that this is a difficult task and that one cannot reasonably be asked to empty oneself of emotional dispositions.

CRITICAL RATIONALISM

So how should inquiry proceed with respect to the question of belief in God? If fideism and strong rationalism are ruled out, what is left is a position that Peterson, Hasker, Reichenbach and Basinger call critical rationalism. According to critical rationalism, religious belief systems can and must be rationally criticized and evaluated, although conclusive proof of such a system is impossible. But while "proof" as understood by the strong rationalist is not the sort of

---

[11]C. S. Lewis, *Miracles: A Preliminary Study* (New York: Macmillan Paperbacks Edition, 1978), especially his opening chapter, pp. 3-5.

proof that ought to be accepted by all rational persons, nonetheless there is a person-relative conception of proof that can be employed within a critical rationalist framework. There are arguments that, given one's own perspective, can provide good reason to believe that God exists or to believe that God does not exist.

Alvin Plantinga, perhaps the world's leading philosopher of religion of the past twenty-five years, has defended the claim that the existence of God is properly basic, by which he means that it can be perfectly rational to believe that God exists without having an argument whereby one can infer the belief that God exists from some other belief.[12] By the same token he does maintain that there are numerous arguments for God's existence. However, the arguments are not necessarily proofs from every point of view, but rather from certain points of view. If the proof is supposed to demonstrate that the argument ought to be persuasive regardless of the viewpoint from which it is evaluated, then Plantinga claims that there are no proofs of the existence of God. If the proof simply provides support for theism given some intellectual predispositions, then he holds that there are two or three dozen such proofs, at a conservative estimate.[13]

But perhaps a critical rationalist perspective is inappropriate for the study of C. S. Lewis's arguments. After all, to many people Lewis comes across as a purveyor of "triumphalistic" apologetics. In *Mere Christianity*, for example, he gives a paragraph-long argument against atheism and then pronounces atheism "too simple." Later on he calls it a boy's philosophy.[14] Before Anscombe's critique, Lewis's argument against naturalism demolished that position in a couple of pages. Critics like John Beversluis have maintained that Lewis con-

---

[12]Alvin Plantinga, "Reason and Belief in God," in *Faith and Rationality: Reason and Belief in God*, ed. Alvin Plantinga and Nicholas Wolterstorff (Notre Dame, Ind.: University of Notre Dame Press, 1983), pp. 16-93.

[13]Alvin Plantinga, "Two Dozen (Or So) Theistic Arguments," The Apologia Project (2003) <http://www.theapologiaproject.org/arguments.html>.

[14]C. S. Lewis, *Mere Christianity* (New York: Macmillan, 1960), pp. 31-39.

sistently implied that his conclusions were the complete and final word on the subject in question. Beversluis states, "My complaint about the Broadcast Talks is not that Lewis fails to be as thorough as his subject matter demands, but that he gives the impression of being thorough."[15] Perhaps Lewis's apologetics can be branded a failure simply by pointing out that they failed to accomplish the task he seemed to set for them: thoroughly demolishing all opposition and proving beyond a shadow of a doubt that Christianity is true.

It is quite true that certain passages in Lewis seem to suggest that he believed that his apologetics were designed to satisfy the requirements of strong rationalism. But I believe that the reading of Lewis that fits his writing best as a whole is a reading of him as a critical rationalist. First of all, Lewis's fictional works, such as the Chronicles of Narnia and his Space Trilogy, have noble nonbelievers who do not seem guilty of any irrationality.[16] Second, we find no trace of cognitive pathology in Lewis's account of how the nonbeliever comes not to believe. Although he suggests that perhaps his wish to disbelieve had something to do with his rejecting theism in his early years, he adds:

> But the difficulty of explaining even a boy's thought entirely in terms of his wishes is that on such large questions as these he always has wishes on both sides. Any conception of reality which a sane mind can admit must favor some of his wishes and frustrate others. The materialistic universe had one great, negative attraction for me. It had no other.[17]

In his essay "On Obstinacy of Belief," Lewis explicitly takes the view that "there is evidence both for and against the Christian prop-

---

[15]Beversluis, C. S. Lewis and the Search, p. 42. For a discussion of the charge of triumphalism, see Scott R. Burson and Jerry L. Walls, C. S. Lewis and Francis Schaeffer: Lessons for a New Century from the Most Influential Apologists of Our Time (Downers Grove, Ill.: InterVarsity Press, 1998), pp. 239-44.
[16]Trumpkin, the dwarf who remains skeptical about Aslan throughout Prince Caspian, and MacPhee, the skeptical friend of Ransom in That Hideous Strength, are good examples.
[17]C. S. Lewis, Surprised by Joy (San Diego, Calif.: Harcourt Brace, 1955), p. 172.

ositions which fully rational minds, working honestly, can assess differently."[18] In this essay Lewis refuses to explain his opponents in terms of cognitive pathology.

> There are of course people in our day to whom the whole situation seems altered by the doctrine of the concealed wish. They will admit that men, otherwise apparently rational, have been deceived by the arguments for religion. But they will say that they have been deceived first by their own desires and produced the arguments as a rationalization: that these arguments have never been intrinsically even plausible, but have seemed so because they were secretly weighted by our wishes. Now I do not doubt that this sort of thing happens in thinking about religion as it happens in thinking about other things: but as a general explanation of religious assent it seems to be quite useless. On that issue our wishes may favor either side or both. The assumption that every man would be pleased, if only he could conclude that Christianity is true, appears to me to be simply preposterous. . . . Men wish on both sides, and again, there is fear-fulfillment as well as wish fulfillment. And hypochondriac temperaments will always think true what they most wish to be false. Thus instead of one predicament on which our opponents sometimes concentrate there are in fact four. A man may be a Christian because he wants Christianity to be true. He may be an atheist because he wants atheism to be true. He may be an atheist because he wants Christianity to be true. He may be a Christian because he wants atheism to be true. Surely these possibilities cancel one another out?[19]

But is Lewis really serious about not issuing irrationality charges against his opponents? Beversluis thinks that this claim needs to be taken with a grain of salt, given the triumphalistic tone of much of Lewis's apologetics. He writes:

> In *Miracles* we learn that naturalists contradict themselves and reduce

---

[18]C. S. Lewis, "On Obstinacy of Belief," in *Philosophy of Religion: An Anthology*, ed. Louis Pojman, 3rd ed. (Belmont, Calif.: Wadsworth, 1998), p. 390.
[19]Ibid., p. 390.

human reasoning to an involuntary response "like a hiccup, yawn, or vomit." In *"De Futilitate"* and *"The Poison of Subjectivism"* we discover that ethical subjectivists hold that moral judgments are "mere tastes" and "personal preferences" on the same level as a fondness for pancakes or a dislike for spam." In *The Abolition of Man* we are assured that the heads of these so-called intellectuals seem large only because they have allowed their chests to atrophy. Sometimes they are a laughingstock, as when, having just mocked patriotism, they are shocked to discover traitors in their midst. Lewis mockingly implores those subjectivists who have destroyed his reverence for conscience on Monday not to expect to find him "venerating" it on Tuesday (M, 47). In "Bulverism" we are assured that naturalists prefer "sheer self-contradictory idiocy" to a belief in the powers of reason. Atheists tell lies (even "good, solid resounding lies"), believe that the universe came into existence by a fluke, modify their self-contradictory claims only when compelled to do so, and dishonestly revert to them the moment the crisis has passed.[20]

Beversluis goes on to contend that Lewis's real position is essentially that atheists are irrational, and that any comments that suggest otherwise are somewhat disingenuous. His practice of setting up straw men when presenting atheist (and ethical subjectivist) positions is proof that he regards their positions as simply foolish.

Now I should say that these quotations, for various reasons, leave us with a distorted picture of Lewis's attitude toward unbelief, as well as toward people committed to other positions Lewis criticizes, such as ethical subjectivism. To a large extent Beversluis is here confusing what Lewis is saying about the logical *implications* of a position with what he thinks people who hold the position *actually believe.* I might think that to be fully consistent, a materialist should be an eliminativist about truth and an eliminativist about beliefs. I am inclined to suppose that materialism pushed to its logical conclusion leads to eliminativism, that is, to the conclusion that there is no truth and that there are

---

[20]Beversluis, *C. S. Lewis and the Search*, pp. 87-88.

no beliefs. Does that mean that I think that all materialists have drawn such a conclusion? No, only Paul and Patricia Churchland and their followers have drawn this conclusion. I think that these conclusions really do follow from materialism, however unwilling materialists might be to draw them. However, I also think a rational and intelligent materialist might in fact fail to draw them, because they have over-looked something or because they come to the discussion with a deeply rooted conviction that materialism must be true. They may be just as sure that there are beliefs and on that account conclude that any argument purporting to show that there can't be beliefs in a materialist universe must have something wrong with it.

There is an important difference between the reductio ad absurdum arguments that we find in Lewis and others on the one hand and the straw man fallacy on the other. If arguments are provided for the conclusion that a position has absurd consequences, this is not the straw man fallacy. Only when the straw man is presented without any arguments showing why these conclusions follow from a position actually held does one commit the straw man fallacy.

Second, sometimes major advocates of the positions criticized by Lewis state their own position in ways that Beversluis would regard as committing the straw man fallacy. Beversluis seems to think it an instance of the straw man fallacy to attribute to the ethical subjectiv-ist the view that moral judgments are mere tastes on a level with a liking for pancakes and a dislike for Spam, but I wonder what he would make of Bertrand Russell, who wrote:

> The theory which I have been advocating is a form of the doctrine which is called the "subjectivity" of values. This doctrine consists in maintaining that, if two men differ about values, there is not a dis-agreement as to any kind of truth, but a difference of taste. If one man says "oysters are good" and another says "I think they are bad," we rec-ognize that there is nothing to argue about. The theory in question holds that all differences as to values are of this sort, although we do

not naturally think them so when we are dealing with matters that seem to us more exalted than oysters.[21]

While subsequent ethical subjectivists may not have found this comparison with taste in food a good analogy to describe their position, major figures like Russell and A. J. Ayer did describe their own view in just the way that Beversluis refers to as a straw man.

In addition, some of the comments Beversluis attributes to Lewis appear to be comments not about what all unbelievers say and do, but only about what some say and do. Lewis seems to hold nonbelievers to the high standard of intellectual integrity set by his tutor Kirkpatrick (who is reincarnated in the character MacPhee in *That Hideous Strength*) and often expresses disappointment when actual nonbelievers fail to live up to that standard. But this does not provide any reason to suppose that Lewis viewed all unbelievers as deserving to be laughingstocks.

Nevertheless, Beversluis's comments point us in the direction of something very important about Lewis. I think there is a persistent inner tension between two voices in Lewis's writings, the voice of the confident apologist and the Christian agnostic. The confident apologist makes strong, bold claims on behalf of Christianity. The Christian agnostic raises tough questions and refuses to let the solutions be too easy. I think that both voices are genuinely Lewis's and that an authentic reading of Lewis's apologetics requires close attention to both. Lewis is appealing as an apologist partly because he boldly presents arguments on behalf of Christianity, but he is also appealing because he is able to understand why someone would have doubts about Christianity. I find many Christian expositors and apologists frustrating because they make believing a little bit too easy, and also

---

[21]Bertrand Russell, "Science and Ethics," originally published in Russell, *Religion and Science* (Oxford: Oxford University Press, 1961), posted at <http://www.luminary.us/russell/science-ethics.html>.

because they paper over problems that need to be taken more seriously than they are.

In Lewis we sometimes get the "short version" of certain arguments on behalf of Christianity, but at other times Lewis is as good as a skeptic at pointing out difficulties. In the beginning of *The Problem of Pain* we find a presentation of the argument from evil, which surely rivals what we find in David Hume and Bertrand Russell.[22] While most people pass over it, Lewis specifically points out that in the Twenty-third Psalm the psalmist mentions the table is spread before him in the presence of his enemies, implying that what makes the spreading of the table great is that his enemies are looking on enviously, reflecting a vengeful attitude apparently at odds with the New Testament.[23] He devotes an essay to a problem about petitionary prayer called "Petitionary Prayer: A Problem Without an Answer."[24] When Charles Williams likens writers of books like *The Problem of Pain* to the comforters of Job, Lewis accepts the point and incorporates it into his treatments of the issue in subsequent writings.[25] The entire first section of *Till We Have Faces* is dedicated to a complaint by the main character of the book against "the gods."[26]

Those who find *A Grief Observed* to be a radical departure from previous apologetic writings have failed to observe in Lewis's writings this recurring theme that we might call "creative" questioning of God. Beversluis notices Lewis the Christian agnostic in "On Obstinacy in Belief" and in *A Grief Observed*, but a close study reveals C. S. Lewis the Christian agnostic in virtually all of Lewis's writings.

[22]C. S. Lewis, *The Problem of Pain* (New York: Macmillan Paperbacks Edition, 1962), pp. 13-15.
[23]C. S. Lewis, *Reflections of the Psalms* (San Diego, Calif.: Harcourt Brace Jovanovich, 1958), pp. 20-33.
[24]C. S. Lewis, "Petitionary Prayer: A Problem Without an Answer," in *Christian Reflections* (Grand Rapids, Mich.: Eerdmans, 1967), pp. 142-51.
[25]C. S. Lewis, ed., *Essays Presented to Charles Williams* (Grand Rapids, Mich.: Eerdmans, 1974), p. xiii.
[26]C. S. Lewis, *Till We Have Faces* (San Diego, Calif.: Harcourt Brace Jovanovich, 1956).

To forcefully and confidently present reasons why one believes something is not the same as assuming that only a fool could believe otherwise. I maintain that Lewis's rhetoric, which I will admit has more of a triumphalist tone than I would myself like, nonetheless is quite consistent with the acceptance of critical rationalism, which we find in "On Obstinacy in Belief." In short, I am persuaded that in spite of certain passages that possess a triumphalistic tone, Lewis is best read as a critical rationalist rather than a strong rationalist. But if he was not himself a critical rationalist, his arguments can surely be adapted to the framework of critical rationalism.

I will claim that Lewis's arguments from reason are good arguments in the sense that they provide substantial grounds for rejecting naturalism about the universe and materialism about the mind, and hence a reason for preferring theism about the universe and dualism or some other nonmaterialist view about the mind. If successful, that will be a good day's work for a philosopher. The argument need not be decisive for all reasonable persons. I will claim, however, that they contribute significantly to a case for theism, so that if someone has not considered these arguments before, they should make it more likely to him or her that theism is true than it would have been without considering them.

THREE

C. S. Lewis, Elizabeth Anscombe and the Argument from Reason

"WHEN WE HEAR OF SOME NEW ATTEMPT to explain reasoning or language or choice naturalistically, we ought to react as if we were told that someone had squared the circle or proved the square root of 2 to be rational. Only the mildest curiosity is in order—how well has the fallacy been concealed?"[1]

There are various phenomena to which believers in the existence of God can appeal in support of the claim that God exists. Theists have looked to the beginning of the universe, to the design of the universe, to our moral experience, to evidence in support of miracles and to religious experience in order to ground the belief that God does exist. One phenomenon that is sometimes neglected in the development of theistic arguments is the existence of rational thought. Does our very thinking provide evidence that theism is true?

The argument I will be presenting in this book will attempt to answer that question in the affirmative. This argument is often advanced against materialism or determinism. For example, the argument is employed against materialism in the writings of Kant.[2]

---

[1]Peter Geach, *The Virtues* (Cambridge: Cambridge University Press, 1977), p. 52. Ironically, Geach was married to the late Elizabeth Anscombe, who is famous for her critique of Lewis's version of the Argument from Reason. Interestingly enough, a well-known Anglo-American philosopher (who did not want to be mentioned by name because he wasn't sure) once told me that he thought Geach agreed with Lewis, not his wife, in this controversy. This passage strongly suggests that he accepted the conclusion of Lewis's argument, in spite of Anscombe's criticisms.

[2]For a discussion of the Kantian foundations of this argument, see H. Allison, "Kant's Refutation of Materialism," *The Monist* 79 (April 1989): 190-209.

However, it was developed as an argument for accepting theism as opposed to naturalism in the last century by British Prime Minister Arthur Balfour,[3] and in the 1940s by Lewis.[4] It was this argument that Elizabeth Anscombe criticized in her famous encounter with Lewis at the Oxford Socratic Club,[5] and as a result Lewis revised his argument in the second edition of his book *Miracles*. Contemporary philosophers who have employed this argument against physical determinism include James Jordan and William Hasker.[6] Those who have developed it into an argument explicitly for theism include Richard Purtill and J. P. Moreland.[7] More recently, Alvin Plantinga has defended a version of this argument.[8] Following John Beversluis, a critic of the argument, I will refer to this argument as the argument from reason.[9]

Naturalism is the view that the natural world is all there is and that there are no supernatural beings. Whatever takes place in the universe takes place through natural processes and not as the result of

---

[3]Arthur Balfour, *The Foundations of Belief: Notes Introductory to the Study of Theology*, 8th ed. Rev. with a new introduction and summary (New York: Longmans, 1906), pp. 279-85.

[4]Lewis's argument is found in C. S. Lewis, *Miracles: A Preliminary Study* (New York: Macmillan Paperbacks Edition, 1978), pp. 12-24.

[5]Anscombe's critique of the first edition is found in G. E. M. Anscombe, *The Collected Papers of G. E. M. Anscombe*, 3 vols. (Minneapolis: University of Minnesota Press, 1981), pp. 224-31. A previous discussion of mine on that exchange is found in Victor Reppert, "The Lewis-Anscombe Controversy: A Discussion of the Issues," *Christian Scholar's Review* 19 (September 1989): 32-48.

[6]James Jordan, "Determinism's Dilemma," *Review of Metaphysics* 23 (1969-1970): 48-66; William Hasker, "The Transcendental Refutation of Determinism," *Southern Journal of Philosophy* 11 (1973): 175-83; *Metaphysics* (Downer's Grove, Ill.: InterVarsity Press, 1983); and "Why the Physical Isn't Closed," chapter 3 of *The Emergent Self* (Ithaca, N.Y.: Cornell University Press, 1999), pp. 58-80.

[7]Richard Purtill, *Reason to Believe* (Grand Rapids, Mich.: Eerdmans, 1974), pp. 44-46; J. P. Moreland, "God and the Argument from Mind," in *Scaling the Secular City* (Grand Rapids, Mich.: Baker, 1987), pp. 77-105.

[8]Alvin Plantinga, *Warrant and Proper Function* (New York: Oxford University Press, 1993), pp. 216-37. Plantinga acknowledges the similarity between his argument and Lewis's in the book's final footnote.

[9]John Beversluis, *C. S. Lewis and the Search for Rational Religion* (Grand Rapids, Mich.: Eerdmans, 1985), pp. 58-83.

supernatural causation. The most popular kind of naturalism is known as materialism or physicalism. Materialism maintains that the basic substances of the physical world are pieces of matter, and physicalism maintains that those pieces of matter are properly understood by the discipline of physics. Some people have suggested that someone who believes in the existence of, say, propositions, which do not have any spatio-temporal location, would be a naturalist but not a materialist. For our purposes a worldview counts as naturalistic if it posits a causally closed "basic level of analysis," and if all other levels have the characteristics they have in virtue of those the basic level has. If the base level is mechanistic but is not composed of matter, then we would have naturalism without materialism. If we have a basic level that is composed of matter but is not to be described by physics (I'm not sure how that's possible), then we have materialism without physicalism. However, if the argument that I am proposing works against physicalism, it will work against nonphysicalist forms of naturalism as well.

Now let us consider the universe from the point of view of physicalism. Suppose, as science has told us, that the universe began with a big bang. The big bang produced material substances of various kinds. And material substances go where they go, not for any purpose, but because the laws of physics mandate such a motion. If rocks fall down a mountain due to an avalanche, they will not stop because they don't want to hit and kill any people. On the mechanistic view of the world, material particles can, through evolution, organize themselves into complicated systems that work together to further the survival of the organism and the species. That is, your eye is structured, through centuries of evolution, in such a way that it serves the function of your seeing. But the particles that make up the eye are, in the mechanistic view, just as mechanistically determined as are the particles of a rock falling down a mountain. What we call "drawing an inference" must be explained in just the same way. Perhaps our brains are structured in such a way that the activity that we call "rational inference" will be performed, and that this capacity contributes to our survival individually and collectively. But the description of this activity as a rational inference is not the description of this activity on the most basic level of analysis. The most basic level of analysis is that of physics, which makes no reference to purposes or logic whatsoever. At that point we've broken things down as far as possible, and we have reached the "basic stuff" of the universe.

To understand what we mean by "the most basic level of analysis," the following passage from Keith M. Parsons' book *God and the Burden of Proof* is helpful. Here Parsons is explicating Richard Swinburne's "powers and liabilities" view of the laws of nature.

> Hence, for Swinburne, to say that a law of nature is unexplained is to say that there is no explanation of how a certain material body possesses the particular powers and liabilities that it has. Of course, the powers and liabilities of one body may be explained in terms of the constituent bodies and those in turn by even more fundamental entities. Presumably, though, rock bottom is eventually reached. At present, rock bottom would be the powers and liabilities of such entities as quarks and electrons. . . . To say that there is no explanation of why a quark, given that it is a fundamental particle, has the powers and liabilities it possesses, seems tantamount to saying that there is no explanation of why a quark is a quark. Surely, anything with different powers and liabilities would not be a quark.[10]

Daniel Dennett, in his essay "Why the Law of Effect Will Not Go Away," presents the commitment to mechanistic explanations as follows:

> Psychology of course must not be question-begging. It must not explain intelligence in terms of intelligence, for instance by assuming

---

[10]Keith Parsons, *God and the Burden of Proof* (Amherst: Prometheus, 1989), pp. 91-92.

responsibility for the existence of intelligence to the munificence of an intelligent creator, or by putting clever homunculi at the control panels of the nervous system. If that were the best psychology could do, then psychology could not do the job assigned to it.[11]

Similarly, Dennett explains the appeal of the Darwinian theory on the grounds that

> Darwin explains a world of final causes and teleological laws with a principle that is independent of "meaning" and "purpose." [Evolutionary theory] assumes a world that is absurd in the existentialist's sense of the term: not ludicrous or pointless, and this assumption is a necessary condition of any non-question-begging account of purpose.[12]

Now it is necessary to be careful about what kinds of "purpose" can exist in a physicalist universe. One can say that the purpose of the heart is to pump blood through the human body. What that must mean is that a conglomeration of particles that pumps blood through the body has the structure it has because having that structure is essential for the ability of the organism to survive. So without an actual intended purpose, a heart can have the purpose (that is, function) of pumping blood. And that function is a Darwinian byproduct. "Meaning" and "reasoning" must have the same type of explanation. There are physical processes that are evolutionary byproducts, the idea being that structures that serve their purposes can be explained in Darwinian terms, but in the final analysis the explanation must be mechanistic. In the last analysis the purposes must be explained in terms of the nonpurposive.

This is the exact opposite of what we find in theism, where the apparently nonpurposive order of the physical world is explainable in terms of the intentions and purposes of God. In contrast to natural-

---

[11]Daniel Dennett, "Why the Law of Effect Will Not Go Away," *Journal for the Theory of Social Behavior* 5, no. 2 (1976): 171.
[12]Ibid., pp. 171-72.

ism, theism maintains that the universe is rational because God, a rational being, created it. Reason, on the theist view, is on the ground floor of reality. Given that God creates creatures, it is at least possible that God might wish to provide those creatures with some measure of the rationality that God possesses. And human beings reflect God's rational character by having the capacity to think logically. Suppose that we make the further supposition that God has created human beings in such a way that they consist of a soul and a body, or in some other way that permits us to transcend determination by physical law. We might then be able to say that while the body's activities are determined (insofar as they are determined at all) by the laws of physics and by antecedent physical conditions, it is possible for human beings, through our souls, to perceive not only the physical activities of the environment, but also logical and mathematical truths that apply throughout all that God has created. If someone in a theistic universe who has a spiritual as well as a physical nature reasons to a conclusion logically, this might occur, in the final analysis, because the person perceives that the conclusion follows from the premises. It need not be, in the final analysis, because the laws of physics mandated that the physical particles in the brain move to such and such places.

MATERIALISM, PHYSICALISM AND NATURALISM

When C. S. Lewis presented the argument from reason in his revised third chapter of *Miracles*, he claimed that what he called "strict materialism" could be refuted by a one-sentence argument that he quoted from J. B. S. Haldane: "If my mental processes are determined wholly by the motions of atoms in my brain, I have no reason to suppose that my beliefs are true . . . and hence I have no reason for supposing my brain to be composed of atoms."[13] However, Lewis

---

[13]Lewis, *Miracles*, p. 15. Lewis quoted from J. B. S. Haldane, *Possible Worlds* (1927; reprint, New Brunswick, N.J.: Transaction Publishers, 2001).

maintains that naturalism involves the same difficulty, but he goes on for nine pages explaining why. I suspect that in Lewis's time the idea of nonreductive materialism was not as prevalent as it has since become, and that what passed as "materialism" was identified with strong forms of reductionism. However, here I will be defining materialism broadly, such that it will be very difficult for someone to argue that some form of nonmaterialist naturalism will escape the difficulties I advance for materialism.

Any genuinely naturalistic position requires that all instances of explanation in terms of reasons be further explained in terms of a nonpurposive substratum. For if some purposive or intentional explanation can be given and no further analysis can be given in nonpurposive and nonrational terms, then reason must be viewed as a fundamental cause in the universe, and this strikes me as a huge concession to positions such as theism, idealism and pantheism, which maintain that reasons are fundamental to the universe. Any genuinely naturalistic position will be subject to the same objections that I am presenting against materialism, so I will develop my argument in relation to materialism.

There are three forms of materialism that are discussed and defended by philosophers today. Some forms of materialism maintain that since materialism is true, we should accept the existence of only those mental states that can be found in the brain. If, for instance, beliefs cannot be found in the brain, then the conclusion to draw is not that they exist in the nonphysical mind, but that they do not exist at all. According to eliminative materialists like Paul Churchland, the claim that beliefs and desires exist presupposes the truth of a false theory, which they call folk psychology. Human rationality, in the eliminativist's view, is described by the ultimate brain theory in terms that do not include propositional attitudes. A second type of materialism maintains that mental states are reducible to physical states. A third type of materialism maintains that mental states are not identical to, but rather are supervenient on physical states. Mental states are determined by physical states, and given the state of the physical, there is only one way the mental can be.[14] On this view, mental states may not be physical states, but there are no differences among mental states without corresponding physical differences. Any possible world that differs from this one in any other way differs from this one in a physical way. If there are two possible worlds, and Jones is thinking about his Aunt Maude in one and his Aunt Frances in another, then there must be some aspect of the physical world that is different and that explains the difference between those two worlds.

Defenders of each of the three versions of materialism, however, can agree with the following definition.

1. The physical level is to be understood mechanistically, such that purposive explanations must be further explained in terms of a non-purposive substratum. This will be called the mechanism thesis.

2. The physical order is causally closed. No nonphysical causes operate on the physical level. The physical level is a comprehensive system of events that is not affected by anything that is not itself physical. This is called the causal closure thesis.

3. Other states, such as mental states, (if they exist) supervene on physical states. Given the state of the physical, there is only one way the mental, for example, can be. This is the supervenience thesis.[15] Sometimes this is called the supervenience and determination thesis. The idea is that the state of the supervening state is guaranteed by the state of the supervenience base. Thus it might be argued that biological states supervene upon physical and chemical states. Imagine a scenario in which a mountain lion

---

[14]A vast literature has accumulated on the topic of mental-physical supervenience theory. See especially Jaegwon Kim, *Supervenience and Mind: Selected Philosophical Essays* (Cambridge: Cambridge University Press, 1991).

[15]This tripartite definition of materialism or physicalism is based on William Hasker's discussion in *Emergent Self*, pp. 59-64.

kills and eats a deer. Even though "mountain lion" and "deer" are not physical terms, nevertheless, given the physical state of the world, it cannot be false that a mountain lion is killing a deer.

All of these claims are compatible with eliminative, reductive and nonreductive materialism. Of course, reductive and eliminative materialists will insist that there are no irreducible states that merely supervene on the physical. But such states at least supervene on the physical, and so the reductive and eliminative materialist need not reject this definition of their position. These doctrines are not tendentiously defined in such a way as to make physicalism easy to attack. Rather, these doctrines represent a consensus understanding among physicalists of various stripes about what physicalism involves.

It has sometimes been suggested that although the argument from reason is perhaps an argument against materialism or physicalism, it is nonetheless not an argument against naturalism. But as I have noted, materialism/physicalism is a form of naturalism in which the basic level of analysis is the physical level. Naturalism can include philosophies in which there is no such thing as matter per se, or in which the base level is not physics. But this does not mean that purposive basic explanations can be admitted into a naturalist's worldview. The argument from reason first argues that if we are capable of rational inference, then the basic explanation for some events in the universe must be given in terms of reasons, not in terms of the blind operation of nature obeying the laws of nature. Only subsequently does the argument attempt to show that theism (or some other mentalistic metaphysical system) best accounts for this explanatory dualism.

Further, some have suggested that the existence of abstract entities, while perhaps not consistent with strict physicalism, can resolve the naturalist's problem. The idea is that in addition to physical states there can exist, consistent with naturalism, abstract entities such as propositions, states of affairs and so forth that do not have any particular spatial or temporal location and that exercise no causal power.

Nevertheless, when one has a belief, one believes a proposition to be true. But even if we grant that these abstract states are consistent with naturalism, I fail to see that this can possibly help the naturalist account for reasoning. Whatever the abstract state is, that state must in some way be capable of affecting the way beliefs in the world of space-time are produced and sustained. And if physics is a closed system, then it seems impossible for abstract entities, even if they exist, to make any difference in how beliefs are caused. So I see no escape along these lines for the naturalist.

FORMULATING THE ARGUMENT FROM REASON — WITH HELP FROM ANSCOMBE

Very well, then, how can we formulate the argument from reason in such a way that it is most effective and open to the fewest misunderstandings? In the first edition of *Miracles*, C. S. Lewis presents an argument that goes as follows:

1. No thought is valid if it can be fully explained as the result of irrational causes.

2. If materialism is true, then all thoughts can be fully explained as the result of irrational causes.

3. Therefore, if materialism is true, then no thought is valid.

4. If no thought is valid, then the thought "materialism is true" is not valid.

5. Therefore, if materialism is true, then the thought "materialism is true" is not valid.

6. A thesis whose truth entails the invalidity of the thought that it is true ought to be rejected, and its denial ought to be accepted.

7. Therefore, materialism ought to be rejected, and its denial ought to be accepted.

Now premise 6 of this argument seems eminently plausible. That is, there do indeed seem to be propositions whose truth invalidates them as rational beliefs. For example, if I maintained that no one is ever persuaded by an argument, that those who pretend to be persuaded by arguments are in fact being persuaded by irrational causes of, say, a Freudian nature, then I could not, of course, hope to persuade someone of this by an argument, because I could only succeed if my argument failed.

When Lewis talks about the validity of reason, he is talking about something broader than deductive validity, and this has led to some confusion on the part of some commentators. So perhaps it might be better to substitute something more familiar in the theory of knowledge, the idea of a justified belief. Presumably our epistemic goals are met by beliefs that can be both true and justified; indeed the traditional definition of knowledge is justified true belief. If the truth of one's belief makes it unjustified, this surely would make the belief a prime candidate for rejection.

So we can reformulate the argument as follows:

1. No belief is justified if it can be fully explained as the result of irrational causes.

2. If materialism is true, then all beliefs can be explained as the result of irrational causes.

3. Therefore, if materialism is true, then no belief is justified.

4. If materialism is true, then the belief "materialism is true" is not justified.

5. Therefore, materialism should be rejected.

Why should one believe that no belief is justified if it can be fully explained as the result of irrational causes? Lewis points out that we typically assume this when we attempt to find irrational causes for the beliefs of our opponents as a way of discrediting their beliefs. For example, many people suppose that beliefs that are the products of our wishes cannot be justified. Why? Because our wishes are not a good index of the way things are, and they are as likely to produce false beliefs as true beliefs. What we wish for might be true, but the fact that we wish it were true does not, in the ordinary case, make it true.

But why should one suppose that if naturalism is true, then all beliefs can be explained as the result of irrational causes? One of Elizabeth Anscombe's criticisms of Lewis's argument concerns precisely this claim.[16] Anscombe's contention was that Lewis conflated all nonrational causes with irrational causes. Irrational causes tend to produce false beliefs where rational causes ought to be operating; nonrational causes are simply physical events. An irrational cause, for example, is someone's belief that all black dogs are dangerous because that person was bitten by one as a child. Now naturalism, as explicated in terms of supervenient materialism, seems committed to the belief that all beliefs can be explained as the result of nonrational causes, but it is not committed to the view that all beliefs can be explained as the result of irrational causes.

This is a fair criticism; at least Lewis thought is was sufficiently fair to warrant revising the argument to talk about nonrational rather than irrational causes. But does this really resolve the materialist's problem? We might begin by noting that the credibility of materialism rests to a very large extent on the credibility of the natural sciences, and these sciences seem to be crucially dependent, in turn, upon mathematics and logic. What is more, naturalistic philosophers often present logical arguments to defend their position or to criticize opposing positions. Now arguments are designed to cause others to draw inferences, but drawing inferences seems to require a rational cause for beliefs, not merely the absence of irrational causes. The argument from reason, as I understand it, should be understood

---

[16]G. E. M. Anscombe, *Metaphysics and the Philosophy of Mind*, vol. 2 of *The Collected Papers of G. E. M. Anscombe* (Minneapolis: University of Minnesota Press, 1981), pp. 224-25.

as the argument from rational inference.

Lewis makes the statement that all knowledge depends on the validity of reasoning, which has suggested to some commentators that his argument depends on commitment to inferential theories of perceptual knowledge, with the subsequent implication that if inferential theories are rejected, then the argument from reason must be also.[7] Some philosophers have maintained that when I see a blue marker in my hand, I am directly aware of my own sensation of having a blue-markerish sense datum, and I infer the existence of a real blue marker from my visual sensations. Other philosophers say that I am directly aware of the real blue marker without drawing any inferences. However, the argument can be formulated in such a way as to avoid any commitment to such inferential theories. The reason this can be done is that we know that naturalists depend crucially on rational inference to provide the logical and mathematical foundations of the natural sciences, and they rely on inference when they defend their own beliefs. That being the case, they must accept the idea that at least some beliefs are inferred from other beliefs, and if it can be shown that their position rules out the possibility of rational inference, then that would provide a very powerful reason to reject naturalism.

So let us formulate the argument once again:

1. No belief is rationally inferred if it can be fully explained in terms of nonrational causes.

2. If materialism is true, then all beliefs can be fully explained in terms of nonrational causes.

---

[7] See especially Beversluis, *C. S. Lewis and the Search*, pp. 80-81. Beversluis accuses Lewis of inconsistently using experiential data after saying that all our knowledge depends on the *validity* of reasoning. And this, he says, leaves Lewis with no way to defend his belief in an external world. But of course Lewis does not need to deny, and does not deny, the legitimacy of experiential knowledge, and what he says seems perfectly compatible with the idea that we perceive physical objects directly, without performing inferences in so doing.

3. Therefore, if materialism is true, then no belief is rationally inferred.

4. If any thesis entails the conclusion that no belief is rationally inferred, then it should be rejected and its denial accepted.

5. Therefore materialism should be rejected and its denial accepted.

Anscombe makes another criticism that is important to understanding the nature of the argument. According to Anscombe, the way one would explain or acquire the concept of validity (or rational inference for that matter) is by contrasting paradigm cases of valid and invalid reasoning. She says that Lewis might respond by saying that even though we do acquire the concept of validity by contrasting paradigm cases of valid and invalid reasoning, if materialism were true the distinction between valid and invalid reasoning would be destroyed, because if materialism were true we would have no reason to suppose that what we called valid was really valid. But, she asks, "What *can* you mean by valid beyond what would be indicated by the explanation you give for distinguishing between valid and invalid reasoning, and what in the (materialistic) hypothesis prevents the explanation from being given or from meaning what it does?"[18]

Anscombe here is employing the paradigm case argument, an argument against the possibility of meaningfully raising certain skeptical questions. Suppose someone were to advance, as Descartes did, the possibility that we are systematically being deceived about everything by an omnipotent evil demon. According to the paradigm case argument, asking that kind of a question does not make sense, because our language of "truth" and "falsity" makes sense within a rule-governed linguistic activity (to use Wittgenstein's term, a language game) whereby we distinguish true beliefs from false beliefs. Only

[18] Anscombe, *Metaphysics*, p. 226.

when we have paradigm cases of true beliefs and false beliefs does it make sense to ask which are true and which are false. To ask, *Could all my beliefs be false?* would be, according to the argument, to ask a nonsense question.

According to the paradigm case argument (as applied to the issue at hand) we could tell the difference between valid and invalid reasoning only if we had drawn a contrast between paradigm cases of each. So it does not make sense to argue that if materialism were true, there would be no valid arguments. Anscombe interprets Lewis's argument from the first edition as asking the question of whether all our inferences could be invalid, and as such she is arguing that it can be refuted by a paradigm case argument.

If the argument from reason is presented as a skeptical threat argument, then I believe it does fall prey to a paradigm case argument. For example, suppose I were to argue that materialism cannot be accepted because, if materialism were true, we would not be able to refute skeptics concerning the basic principles of logic. Then the materialist could respond that it is neither necessary nor possible to refute someone who is skeptical of the basic principles of logic. But if someone should take up the burden of proving that these principles of logic are true, then it will simply be impossible to prove their validity. Any argument that is offered to bear that burden of proof will invariably presuppose exactly the principles that are at issue and will hence be question-begging in much the way that, as Hume pointed out, attempts to appeal to experience to defend the basic principles of induction will invariably beg the question. This is a difficulty that the naturalist and the supernaturalist share equally. If one tried to argue that appeal to God's benevolence could refute the logical skeptic and tried to formulate that into an argument, then one would presuppose the correctness of basic logical principles in so doing and thereby beg the question. Neither side can refute a skeptic about the basic principles of logic, but both must assume the legitimacy of those principles in order to argue at all.

The alternative way to present the argument from reason, then, is to begin with the premise that rational inference occurs and that if this is so, then materialism must be false. It is not necessary to raise the question of whether there is such a thing as reasoning: we must presuppose that there is. The problem arises in reconciling the fact of reasoning with materialism. If the materialist wishes to say that we are not entitled simply to presume that rational inference occurs, then we can point out the disastrous epistemological consequences involved in denying rational inference. We should note that these consequences do not result from being unable to refute an across-the-board skepticism, but only from materialist assumptions. The skeptical challenge can only be dealt with by insisting that the reliability of our cognitive faculties must simply be assumed.[19] But the best explanation argument maintains that this assumption that our cognitive faculties are reliable has metaphysical consequences; if materialism is assumed, then the assumption cannot be made. Thus we have a good reason to reject materialism.

ANSCOMBE'S TETRACHOTOMY

The bulk of Anscombe's criticisms, however, concern her contention that the argument from reason, at least as presented in Lewis's first edition, fails to distinguish between various types of "full" explanations. Anscombe claimed that "full" explanations are explanations that completely satisfy an inquirer's curiosity, so there can be different "full" explanations depending on what the inquirer wants to know.

Anscombe distinguishes four types of explanations:

---

[19]For a detailed discussion of the Skeptical Threat–Best Explanation distinction, see Reppert, "Lewis-Anscombe Controversy," and Hasker, *Emergent Self*, pp. 68-69.

1. naturalistic causal explanations, typically subsuming the event in question under some physical law

2. logical explanations, showing the logical relationship between the premises and the conclusion

3. psychological explanations, explaining why a person believes as he/she does

4. personal history explanations, explaining how, in the course of someone's personal history, they came to hold a particular belief

Anscombe's criticism of Lewis is that these are four different types of explanation, and that Lewis simply assumes that if explanations of type 1 are given for someone's believing something, then no explanations of type 2, 3 and 4 can possibly be true. But since these are explanations of different types, we have no reason to assume that they are incompatible with one another.

Now explanations of type 2 seem not to be in conflict with explanations of type 1. That is, if something is presented that fits the form of *modus ponens* (an argument form known in logic to be valid), then the fact that it is the result of nonrational causes seems not to affect the validity of the argument. The assessment of the argument's validity seems independent of the causes that produced it. But if wind-blown leaves were to spell out the premises and conclusion of an argument of the form *modus ponens*, would we continue to regard it as even an argument at all if we truly came to believe that the leaves got to be in that formation because they have randomly blown that way?

A good deal of Anscombe's discussion concerns explanations of type 3, explanations of the reasons why one holds a belief. She claims that this type of explanation is not a causal explanation at all; it is the answer one would sincerely give to the question, "Why do you believe that?" And these reasons might be quite sincere even though they do not explain how a person came originally to hold the position he or she holds. One may, for example, become a Christian because of a dramatic religious experience but remain a Christian not so much because of the experience but because Christianity has remained plausible over the years. Anscombe pushes this idea, arguing that reasons-explanations are not causal explanations (this was typical of Wittgensteinians of the time). Anscombe concludes from this that the claim that naturalistic causes exist for every event does not detract from the fact that a person is rational based on his or her ability to sincerely state a belief in X for reason Y, regardless of what causal claims can be made about that person. As Anscombe puts it:

> It appears to me that if a man has reasons, and they are good reasons, and they are genuinely his reasons, for thinking something—then his thought is rational, whatever causal statements can be made about him.[20]

The claim that in giving a reasons-explanation we are not giving a causal explanation is crucial to the Anscombe critique. If she is correct, then it is not necessary to insist, as Lewis does, that in order for reasoning to be possible there has to be some kind of nonphysical causation at work. This position has certainly had adherents. Jaegwon Kim, a naturalistic philosopher acutely aware of the difficulty, given physicalism, of giving an adequate account of mental causation, at one point said it was "well worth considering" the idea that explanation in terms of reasons are noncausal (though he repudiates the suggestion in subsequent essays).[21] And Keith Parsons, in response to my version of the argument from reason, made a statement very similar to that of Anscombe:

> My own (internalist) view is that if I can adduce reasons sufficient for the conclusion Q, then my belief that Q, is rational. The causal history of the mental states of being aware of Q and the justifying

[20]Anscombe, *Metaphysics*, p. 229.
[21]Kim, *Supervenience*, p. 240 n. 4.

grounds strike me as quite irrelevant. Whether those mental states are caused by other mental states, or caused by physical states, or just pop into existence uncaused, the grounds still justify the claim.[22]

In his revised chapter, "The Cardinal Difficulty of the Naturalist," Lewis does not claim that naturalism implies that all thought is produced by irrational causes. Instead he argues that there are two types of connection, connection by cause and effect and connection by ground and consequent. Both types of connection use the word *because*, but these represent two different types of relationship. If we say, "Grandfather is ill because he ate lobster yesterday," we are giving a cause of Grandfather's illness. If we are told, "Grandfather is ill because he hasn't gotten up yet," we are not talking about the cause of his illness (which antedates his failure to rise early); what we are talking about is the evidence that Grandfather is ill. The former is an example of cause and effect, the latter an example of the ground and consequent relationship. While every event in nature must be related to one another by cause and effect, the premises in a rational inference must be related to the conclusion by the ground and consequent relationship. But, Lewis points out, the presence of a cause and effect account of a belief is often used to show the absence or irrelevance of a ground and consequent relationship.[23]

What is more, if we have a genuine case of rational inference, the perception of a ground and consequent relationship must be relevant to the occurrence of the belief. He asks:

> Even if grounds do exist, what have they got to do with the actual occurrence of belief as a psychological event? If it is an event it must be caused. It must in fact be simply one link in a causal chain which stretches back to the beginning and forward to the end of time. How

[22]Keith Parsons, "Further Reflections on the Argument from Reason," *Philo* 3, no. 1 (2000): 101.
[23]Lewis, *Miracles*, p. 15.

could such a trifle as lack of logical grounds prevent the belief's occurrence, and how could the existence of grounds promote it?[24]

Lewis continues by arguing that the only face-saving account of rational inference would have to be that "just as one way in which a mental event causes a subsequent mental event is by Association . . . so another way in which it can cause it is simply by being a ground for it." More precisely, "One thought can cause another not by being, but by being seen to be, a ground for it."[25] But if naturalism is true, then this type of causation, according to Lewis, is impossible. Events in nature are determined by the previous position of material particles, the laws of nature, and (perhaps) a chance factor. In that situation, according to Lewis, the object that is known determines the positive character of the act of knowing. But in rational inference what we know is a logical connection, and a logical connection is not in any particular spatio-temporal location.

I think that, contrary to Anscombe and Parsons, Lewis is correct in supposing that someone cannot be thought of as rational unless certain claims about how one's beliefs are caused are true. First of all, it seems clear enough that claims that a person is rational require that some counterfactual claims be made about him. If someone believes something for a reason and this is the only reason why that person believes it, then it cannot be the case that he would believe what he believes even if rational grounds were absent. For example, if a prosecutor were to believe that the defendant was guilty on the basis of DNA evidence, what would we think of him if it turned out that he hated the defendant so much that he would believe in his guilt regardless of the DNA evidence?

If you were to meet a person, call him Steve, who could argue with great cogency for every position he held, you might on that ac-

---

[24]Ibid., p. 16.
[25]Ibid., pp. 16-17.

count be inclined to consider him a very rational person. But suppose it turned out that on all disputed questions Steve rolled dice to fix his positions permanently and then used his reasoning abilities only to generate the best available arguments for those beliefs selected in the above-mentioned random method. I think that such a discovery would prompt you to withdraw from him the honorific title "rational." Clearly the question of whether a person is rational cannot be answered in a manner that leaves entirely out of account the question of how his or her beliefs are produced and sustained.

Any adequate account of the relation between reasons and causes must provide an account of the role that *convincing* plays in our cognitive economy. The idea of being convinced by something seems to imply that reasons are playing a causal role. Anscombe is attempting not merely to distinguish, but to *divorce* reasons-explanations from causal explanations, considering the former to be noncausal explanations. And insofar as she is divorcing these types of explanations, her critique of Lewis is faulty. If reasons cannot be part of the explanation of how we come to hold beliefs as a matter of personal history, then human rationality as we ordinarily understand it simply does not exist.

Now if we admit that rationality does require certain causal claims, perhaps those causal claims can be explained in a physicalistically acceptable way. Anscombe levels this accusation against Lewis:

> You argue that the naturalist hypothesis about human thinking implies that no human thinking is rational in this sense. For if a man produces what purports to be the conclusion of an argument, in order that what he says should be rational he must say it *because* he has reasoned; but the naturalist hypothesis says that he says it *because* of certain natural causes, and if these causes *fully* explain his utterance, if the chain of causes is complete, there is no room for the operation of a man's own reasoning. So someone might say: "If I claimed to be able to kill a man by an act of will, and he died, but his death was fully explained by the fact that someone who had sworn to murder him had shot him through the heart, that

would demolish the claim to have killed him by an act of will.". . . . Your idea appears to be that "*the* explanation" is everywhere the same one definite requirement, as if there is a fixed place for "*the* explanation" so that we can know, when it is filled, that, if it has been correctly filled, the whole subject of "explaining this fact" has been closed.[26]

Anscombe seems to think that the term "full" explanation simply means that the explanation fully answers an inquirer's question concerning some event. And so there can be many explanations for the same event. For example, if we ask, "Why is the soda can sitting on the bookshelf?" I can answer correctly, "Because I put it there yesterday," or "because I wanted it to be recycled," or "because no one has knocked it over," or "because the shelf holds it up," or "because of the law of gravity," or even "because it is cylindrical," which explains why it stays put on the bookshelf and doesn't roll around. We must admit, with Anscombe, the question-relativity of explanations and also that different explanations can be given for the same event.

But how far can the case for explanatory compatibility be pushed? John Beversluis, in his restatement of Anscombe's critique, says this using the string quartets of Beethoven as his example:

> *Fully* means "exhaustively" only from a particular point of view. Hence the psychologist who claims to have fully explicated the quartets from a psychological point of view is not open to the charge of self-contradiction if he announces his plans to attend a musicologist's lecture on them. In music, as in psychology, the presence of non-rational causes does not preclude reasons. In fact, there is *no limit* to the number of explanations, both rational and non-rational, that can be given why Beethoven composed his string quartets. . . . All of these "fully explicate" the composition of his string quartets. But they are not mutually exclusive. They are not even in competition.[27]

---

[26]Anscombe, *Metaphysics*, p. 228.
[27]Beversluis, *C. S. Lewis and the Search*, pp.73-74, emphasis added.

This line of thought, suggested by Anscombe and pushed further by Beversluis, seems to suggest that explanations of one type cannot exclude explanations of another type. But is this really true? First of all, Beversluis's example is flawed in virtue of the fact that what is being discussed here is different aspects of the composition of the quartets. Whereas what is required is unrestricted explanation of the same aspect. The urge to compose them requires a different explanation from the decisions Beethoven made about what melody to compose, how to put the harmony together and so on. If Beethoven was obsessed with writing for string instruments, we still do not know why he chose quartets as opposed to, say, cello solos. So Beversluis's defense of unrestricted explanatory compatibility fails to refute Lewis's argument that one type cannot exclude another type of explanation.

Second, explanatory exclusion seems to be built into the very idea of naturalism. In particular, the very idea of naturalism seems to exclude supernatural explanations. Let us consider a man's death, which is explained on the one hand in terms of a heart attack and on the other hand in terms of a voodoo curse. It might be argued that while the explanation of a heart attack is the correct medical diagnosis, we might ask why the heart attack occurred, and if we ask this question the answer might be because of a voodoo curse. In fact some followers of Wittgenstein have suggested that since the witchcraft explanation and the scientific explanation occur within different language games, there cannot be a conflict between these types of explanation. But Wittgensteinianism is fundamentally an antirealist philosophy, in which the question of which explanation "limns the true and ultimate structure of reality" need not be asked. An antirealist philosophy does not require that the best account of the world be a true account of the way the world really is. But a realist philosophy does require this. Materialism and/or naturalism, however, *is* a realist philosophy in which the question of which explanation is true must be asked.

If we are thinking within a realist framework, then we must consider the ontological commitments of the explanations we give. If we explain the existence of presents under the Christmas tree in terms of Santa Claus having put them there, then we are committed to the claim that Santa Claus exists. So if a materialist says that she believes in materialism because she perceives the reasons for believing it, then I take it that she is committed to the existence of reasons, as well as the existence of the perceptions of reasons. If she is not, at least the naturalist or materialist owes us an explanation as to why those ontological commitments are not being made. If these commitments are being made, however, then she owes us an explanation for how such reasons for believing fit into the materialist world she says we inhabit. If there are difficulties in doing this, then these have to be difficulties for materialism.

Return once again to the claim that a person died because of a voodoo curse. If materialism is true, then this explanation must be excluded. Why? Well, the death had a physical cause, the heart attack. And the heart attack had a cause, and that cause had a cause, and so on (assuming that it was not a function of pure quantum chance) back to the big bang. The voodoo curse introduces a type of explanation that does not fit into a materialist account of how events are caused in the world. And it does not fit because materialists not only say that a materialist explanation can be given for every event, they also claim that the total causal story, from the beginning to the end of the world, can be given in materialist terms. One of the central concepts in the understanding of materialism, as currently understood, is the causal closure thesis, and this at least presents the specter of excluding competing explanations.

In fact, it seems clear enough that the only kind of causation that is allowable in a materialist universe is physical causation. If there is mental causation, it has to be understood as a subspecies of physical causation. It is not enough simply to say that different "full" explanations can be given for the same event. Of course they can. But given the causal closure thesis of materialism, there cannot be causal explanations that require nonmaterialist ontological commitments. The question that is still open is the question of whether the kinds of mental explanations that must be offered in any face-saving account of rational inference are compatible with the limitations placed on causal explanations by materialism. If not, then there is a conflict between the existence of rational inference and materialism. This means that materialism refutes itself if it presents itself as a rationally inferred belief (or a belief that depends crucially on the existence of rational inference).

Anscombe mentions the existence of personal history explanations, which she says are in some sense causal, but she says that they do not conflict with scientific explanations since the causes involved in scientific explanations are linked to causal laws and are justified by appeal to observed regularities, while explanations linked to personal history explanations are not.[28] But this begs the question. It assumes that explanations that are linked to causal laws can compete only with other explanations that are linked to causal laws. If the foregoing analysis is correct, then explaining how a person, as a matter of personal history, came to believe something in a rational way is critical to understanding that person as a rational agent, and Anscombe has not shown how this is possible on materialist assumptions.

Commentators on the Anscombe exchange have often suggested that a decisive blow was struck against Lewis's argument. As I noted in the first chapter, this claim is frequently based on biographical rather than philosophical grounds. Beversluis, however, maintains that "the objections Anscombe raised can be pressed further, and Lewis's revised argument does nothing to meet them."[29] Anscombe herself,

---

[28]Anscombe, *Metaphysics*, p. 230.
[29]Beversluis, *C. S. Lewis and the Search*, p. 73.

when she included her reply to Lewis in a volume of her essays, gives a more modest assessment of the exchange. While she maintains that her objections were effective against the argument of the first edition, she says that Lewis's revised chapter "corresponds more to the depth and difficulty of the problem" than either his original chapter or her response. Nevertheless, she does have some criticisms. She claims that in the revision Lewis reverts to the concept of full explanation that she had criticized. In addition, he does not develop the idea of "an act of knowing determined by what it knows," which she takes to be clearly crucial. Nevertheless she admits that we don't have an answer to the question, asking, "Even if grounds do exist, what have they got to do with the actual occurrence of belief as a psychological event?"[30]

My overall assessment of the Lewis-Anscombe exchange, once we take into consideration the revisions Lewis made in the argument, is also rather modest. Surely Anscombe's objections rightfully lead us to recognize the distinction between irrational and nonrational causes. The paradigm case argument shows, it seems to me, that Lewis's argument ought to be advanced as a best explanation argument and not as a skeptical threat argument. A best explanation argument begins not by calling into question the validity of human reasoning but by assuming that validity as an established fact. Nevertheless, the best explanation argument maintains that the necessary conditions for rationality cannot exist in a naturalistic universe. And Anscombe's analysis of different types of explanations shows that the defender of the argument needs to come to terms with the issue of explanatory compatibility. But Anscombe's claim that reasons-explanations are not causal explanations seems clearly to be incorrect (as I believe that she subsequently came to see) and the claim that explanations of different types cannot possibly exclude one another seems also to be inadequate. If either of these claims were defensible, then

---

[30]Anscombe, *Metaphysics*, pp. ix-x.

Lewis's argument could be thought of as being permanently refuted, but these claims cannot be defended. It seems clear enough that a physicalistically acceptable account of rational inference must perceive the causation involved in rational inference to be an instance of physical causation. While Anscombe has not demonstrated the compatibility of naturalism and rational inference, the defenders of Lewis need to provide a defense of the incompatibility of naturalism and rational inference. Whether this can be done requires some further analysis, which I hope to provide in the chapters that follow.

Several Formulations of the Argument from Reason

IN THIS CHAPTER I ATTEMPT TO SHOW that the argument from reason is indeed not one argument but several. The arguments from reason are arguments for accepting a theistic understanding of the universe as opposed to a naturalistic one. Other worldviews that make reason fundamental to what is real, such as idealism and pantheism, are views that the argument from reason does not attempt to refute.

There are three stages in the defense of all the arguments from reason that I will be presenting below. The first stage, discussed in this chapter, describes a feature of the reasoning process and defends the claim that those processes are essential to our epistemic life. As such they cannot be re-described in such a way as to eliminate their salient characteristics if we are to still have anything like the knowledge necessary in order to assert the truth of the naturalist's worldview. The second stage, the subject of chapter five, attempts to show that in order to fit reasoning into our universe one must accept a dualism of fundamental explanations. That is, in addition to accepting physical explanations for physical events, we must also accept rational explanations as fundamental explanations for rational inferences. The third stage, to be taken up in chapter six, seeks to show that theism (or some mentalistic worldview) is necessary to account for these fundamental explanations.

The reasoning process on which this argument is based is familiar to all of us. It is essential to the process of science, on which the prestige of the naturalist's worldview is grounded. Presumably Charles Darwin performed rational inferences when he supported the thesis of natural selection with the evidence provided by his observations of the finches on the Galapagos Islands. In particular, the entire enterprise of mathematics is a system of rational inferences. Atheist philosophers expect people to be persuaded by the reasoning in the argument from evil. But this involves thinking that the premises are true, seeing that the premises entail the conclusion, and then actually drawing the conclusion. If there are no rational inferences, our mental lives are far from what we all suppose them to be. So it seems very difficult, on the face of things, for naturalists to cheerfully concede that, of course, if their view is correct, rational inference, as we know it, simply does not occur.

But a lot is implied by the claim that someone has rationally inferred one proposition from another. In particular,

1. States of mind have a relation to the world we call intentionality, or about-ness.

2. Thoughts and beliefs can be either true or false.

3. Human beings can be in the condition of accepting, rejecting or suspending belief about propositions.

4. Logical laws exist.

5. Human beings are capable of apprehending logical laws.

6. The state of accepting the truth of a proposition plays a crucial causal role in the production of other beliefs, and the propositional content of mental states is relevant to the playing of this causal role.

7. The apprehension of logical laws plays a causal role in the acceptance of the conclusion of the argument as true.

8. The same individual entertains thoughts of the premises and then draws the conclusion.

9. Our processes of reasoning provide us with a systematically reliable way of understanding the world around us.

THE ARGUMENT FROM INTENTIONALITY

It seems to me that all of these elements of reasoning are prima facie difficult to fit within the framework of philosophical naturalism. Consider, for example, the "about-ness" of thought. Does it make sense to say that one physical state is about another state? C. S. Lewis thought not:

> We are compelled to admit between the thoughts of a terrestrial astronomer and the behaviour of matter several light-years away that particular relation we call truth. But this relation has no meaning at all if we try to make it exist between the matter of the star and the astronomer's brain, considered as a lump of matter. The brain may be in all sorts of relations to the star no doubt: it is in a spatial relation, and a time relation, and a quantitative relation. But to talk of one bit of matter being true about another bit of matter seems to me to be nonsense.[1]

Surely the laws of physics govern these physical states without any reference at all to what they are "about." If we knew all the physical facts about the world, I contend that it would be like watching a silent movie without subtitles. Different scenarios with respect to the meaning of what is going on could be compatible with the same physical state of the world. If two people are watching the same silent movie without subtitles, it is likely that each of them is seeing a somewhat different story line. There is nothing about what each is seeing on the screen that determines that either of them is correct about what is actually going on in the movie. If reality is fundamentally physical, and the state of the physical world does not uniquely determine what meaning a word has, it follows that the word has no determinate meaning. So how could there be any determinate meaning to the words and concepts that we use? W. V. Quine argued that physical information leaves it indeterminate as to what, say, a speaker of a foreign language means by the word *gavagai*. There is no fact of

---

[1]C. S. Lewis, *Christian Reflections* (Grand Rapids, Mich.: Eerdmans, 1967), p. 64.

the matter as to whether the native is referring to "rabbit" or "undetached rabbit parts."[2] But similarly, would not this argument also show that there is no fact of the matter as to what Quine means by *naturalism* when he says "naturalism is true"?

So we might develop the argument as follows:

1. If naturalism is true, then there is no fact of the matter as to what someone's thought or statement is about.

2. But there are facts about what someone's thought is about. (Implied by the existence of rational inference.)

3. Therefore, naturalism is false.

Some philosophers of mind, known as eliminative materialists, maintain that since intentional states will probably not be found in the course of brain science, it follows that there are no intentional states of the human person. So, for instance, eliminative materialists maintain that there are no beliefs. The obvious question that occurs to most people when they hear this sort of thing is to ask, "You expect me to believe that?"

Although advocates of eliminative materialism have argued that the eliminativist position is not really self-refuting, attempts to defend eliminativism against this charge seem not to be successful, as Lynne Baker, William Hasker and I have argued in print.[3] Rather than going into a detailed discussion of this debate, I will just point out that to accept eliminative materialism is to accept something akin to the belief that we are brains in vats, or that in some other way we are massively deceived about everything. If this expedient is necessary to save naturalism from the argument from reason, it is a des-

---

[2] W. V. Quine, *Word and Object* (Cambridge, Mass.: MIT Press, 1960), chaps. 1 and 2.
[3] Lynne Rudder Baker, *Saving Belief* (Princeton, N.J.: Princeton University Press, 1987); Victor Reppert, "Ramsey on Eliminativism and Self-Refutation," *Inquiry* 34 (1991): 499-508; Victor Reppert, "Eliminative Materialism, Cognitive Suicide, and Begging the Question," *Metaphilosophy* 23 (1992): 378-92; and William Hasker, *The Emergent Self* (Ithaca, N.Y.: Cornell University Press, 1999), pp. 1-26.

perate one indeed, one that undermines the foundations of the very
scientific enterprise on which it is based.

THE ARGUMENT FROM TRUTH

Another aspect of rational inference is found in the ability we have
to discriminate truth from falsity. But, as Lewis says, "to talk about
one bit of matter being true of another seems to me to be nonsense."[4]
Some philosophers, on naturalistic grounds, have suggested that the
consistent application of naturalistic methods to our mental lives will
invariably lead to the elimination or replacement of truth as the central category of epistemic appraisal.

Again, those most ruthless in pursuing a naturalistic methodology
in the philosophy of mind are those who are now prepared to abandon the ideal of truth. Consider the words of Paul Churchland:

> If we are ever to understand the dynamics of cognitive activity, there-
> fore, we may have to reconceive our basic unit of cognition as some-
> thing other than the sentence or proposition, and reconceive its virtue
> as something other than truth. . . . The notion of truth, after all, is but
> the central element in a clutch of descriptive and normative theories
> (folk psychology, folk epistemology, folk semantics, classical logic),
> and we can expect conceptual progress here as elsewhere.[5]

Or again Patricia Churchland:

> Boiled down to essentials, a nervous system enables the organism to
> succeed in . . . feeding, fleeing, fighting, and reproducing. The prin-
> ciple [sic] chore of nervous systems is to get the body parts where they
> should be in order that the organism may survive. Improvements in
> sensorimotor control confer an evolutionary advantage: a fancier style
> of representing is advantageous so long as it is geared to the organism's

---

[4]Lewis, *Christian Reflections*, p. 64.
[5]Paul M. Churchland, "On the Ontological Status of Observables," chap. 8 in A *Neuro-
computational Perspective: The Nature of Mind and the Structure of Science* (Cambridge,
Mass.: MIT/Bradford, 1990), pp. 150-51.

way of life and enhances the organism's chances for survival. Truth, whatever that is, takes the hindmost.[6]

In short, some theorists in the philosophy of mind (and in epistemology also) are telling us that we must be prepared to find nothing in the brain that can be true or false, and if such an alarming occurrence take place, the reasonable thing to do would be to deny the existence of truth.

It seems to me, however, that a very heavy price has to be paid by someone who thinks that truth is eliminable. Those who wish to eliminate truth may suppose that they have something better than truth for us to pursue, but in fact no other value is constitutive of that epistemic point of view. One can pursue effective manipulation of the world, or reproductive fitness, or fame, or glory, or sainthood, but these goals are distinct from the purely epistemic goal of gathering as many (or as high of quality) truths as possible. Either truth is our highest epistemic goal and there is a state of the person called "believing truly," or else we have no epistemic goal and we can engage in various cognitive projects without being held to an absolute standard by which those projects can be judged. With the dethronement of truth, the jaws of epistemic relativism open wide, and that relativism is a deadly enemy of the scientific enterprise.

So again we can formulate another version of the argument from reason:

1. If naturalism is true, then no states of the person can be either true or false.

2. Some states of the person can be true or false. (Implied by the existence of rational inference.)

3. Therefore, naturalism is false.

---

[6] Patricia S. Churchland, "Epistemology in the Age of Neuroscience," *Journal of Philosophy* 84 (October 1987): 548.

If naturalists like the Churchlands are right in supposing that (1) is true, but (2) must be accepted in order for the scientific enterprise to be possible, then this argument is successful in showing that (3) is true.

THE ARGUMENT FROM MENTAL CAUSATION

A third aspect of human reasoning that seems essential for the possibility of rational inference is the reality of mental causation or, more precisely, the fact that one mental state can cause another mental state in virtue of its propositional content. Consider the following syllogism:

1. All men are mortal.

2. Socrates is a man.

3. Therefore, Socrates is mortal.

If rational inference is to be possible, it must be the case that someone can come to believe that (3) is true in virtue of one's being in the state of entertaining and accepting (1), entertaining and accepting (2), and that those two states cause the thinker to reach a state of accepting (3). Hence the existence of mental causation seems necessary for the possibility of rational inference. But there seems to be more involved even than the mere existence of mental causation. One mental event must cause another mental event in virtue of the propositional content of those events. If the thought "All men are mortal" is brain state A, and "Socrates is a man" is brain state B, and "Socrates is mortal" is brain state C, and brain states A and B cause brain state C, it might still be the case that the propositional content of these brain states is irrelevant to the way in which they succeed one another in the brain.

Consider the following example. Suppose a baseball used in Sandy Koufax's fourth no-hitter is thrown and hits a window. We might say that a Sandy Koufax baseball was used to shatter the window, but it would not at all follow that that the window broke in virtue of the ball having been used by Sandy Koufax. What determined whether or not the window shattered upon impact is a function of the velocity of the baseball and the strength of the glass, and its use in the no-hitter would be simply irrelevant to the present causal transaction. Whether a computer's activity is interpreted as a chess game or as a word-processing program will not affect the actual output of the computer, though no doubt it will affect the input that its users generate.

What this means is that even if there are intentional states, even if those states can be true or false, it might still be the case that one mental event cannot cause another in virtue of its content. If all causation is physical causation, it might be asked how the content of a mental state could possibly be relevant to what causes what in the world.

A widely held form of nonreductive materialism is a doctrine known as anomalous monism, originally developed by Donald Davidson. According to anomalous monism, mental items can be defined by a special quality, that of intentionality. Thus, mental states can have contents that do not correspond to anything in the material world (e.g. false beliefs). This is a property dualist position, that is, the view that while the mind may not be a separate substance from the physical body, it nonetheless has properties that cannot be described or explained at the level of the physical. This is property dualist because when mental states are wearing their intentional labels, they cannot be fitted into lawlike statements and therefore cannot be predicted or explained by causal laws. Nevertheless, the mental events themselves are nothing more than brain events. On Davidson's view, mental states may be physically caused by other mental states, but they are not caused by the propositional content of the other mental states. This position raises the issue of description versus explanation. In Davidson's view, we have a pluralism of description but not a pluralism of explanation.[7] Consider Jaegwon Kim's comments in response to anomalous monism:

---

[7]This definition is taken from Kevin Silber, "Dualism," *Philosophical Psychology* (2002) <www.staffs.ac.uk/soss/psychology/coursematerials/philpsy/dualism/>.

Davidson's anomalous monism fails to do justice to psychophysical causation in which the mental *qua* mental has any real causal role to play. Consider Davidson's account: whether or not an event has a mental description (optional reading, whether or not it has a mental characteristic) seems entirely irrelevant to the causal relations it enters into. Its causal powers are wholly determined by the physical description or characteristic that holds for it. For it is under its physical description that it may be subsumed under a causal law.[8]

What this means is that on Davidson's view, it cannot be true of a naturalist that he accepts atheism because of the argument from evil, or that he accepts anomalous monism because Davidson's argument for it is strong. In Davidson's view (at least if Kim's charges are correct), though the event "thinking that there is gratuitous evil in the world" can cause the belief "there is no God," it cannot do so in virtue of the propositional content of those beliefs. Hence, if Davidson is right about mental events, one cannot believe this for the reason provided by Davidson himself, or for any other reason.

So still another version of the argument from reason presents itself:

1. If naturalism is true, then no event can cause another event in virtue of its propositional content.

2. But some events do cause other events in virtue of their propositional content. (Implied by the existence of rational inference.)

3. Therefore naturalism is false.

In the previous chapter, I discussed the responses of Anscombe and Parsons that essentially deny mental causation in virtue of content and showed them to be inadequate. It seems clear enough that mental causation in virtue of content is essential for rational inference.

---

[8]Jaegwon Kim, "Epiphenomenal and Supervenient Causation," in *Supervenience and Mind: Selected Philosophical Essays* (Cambridge, Mass.: Cambridge University Press, 1991), p. 106.

THE ARGUMENT FROM THE PSYCHOLOGICAL RELEVANCE OF LOGICAL LAWS

Even if it turns out that a naturalistic worldview can account for causation in terms of mental content, a further problem can be brought forward. Rational inference involves the employment of the laws of logic. These laws are not physical laws. Indeed they pertain across possible worlds, including worlds with no physical objects whatsoever. So while the laws of physics denote the powers and liabilities of things in the physical world, the laws of logic tell us what must be true in any universe whatsoever. Even in possible worlds with no law of gravity, the law of noncontradiction still holds. If one accepts the laws of logic, as one must if one claims to have rationally inferred one belief from another belief, then one must accept some nonphysical, nonspatial and nontemporal reality—at least something along the lines of the Platonic forms.

It is further supposed that we know these laws. But the only acceptable physicalist analysis of knowledge would have to be some kind of causal interaction between the brain and the objects of knowledge. But if we know or have insight into the laws of logic, we must be in some kind of physical relationship to the laws of logic. This is quite impossible if the laws of logic are, as I have contended, nonphysical, nonspatial and nontemporal. The fact that we cannot be causally connected to numbers if they are real is often given as a reason why we should not be realists about numbers.[9] A similar argument could just as easily be advanced for why, if we are going to be naturalists, we should not be realists about the laws of logic. But nonrealism about logical laws has a serious problem, posed long ago by Aristotle.[10] If we are nonrealists about logical laws, that is, if we do not suppose that the laws of logic really exist, then we cannot coherently

---

[9] Paul Benacerraf, "Mathematical Truth," *The Journal of Philosophy* 70, no. 19 (1973): 661-73.
[10] Aristotle, *Metaphysics*, book 4, chap. 4.

assert that this is so, for if we were to do so, we would have to presuppose the legitimacy of those very logical laws (for example, the law of noncontradiction). So philosophical naturalism undermines the laws that are presupposed in the very assertion of philosophical naturalism.

It is often supposed that the laws of logic are true by convention. But this is clearly not a coherent idea. Before conventions can be established, logic must already be presupposed. If logical laws are human conventions, then presumably it is at least possible for us to have had different conventions. But the laws of logic are conditions of intelligibility; without them we could not say anything. Part of what it means to say anything is to imply that the contradictory is false. Otherwise, language simply does not function in a declarative way. So the reality of logical laws cannot be denied without self-refutation, nor can their psychological relevance be denied without self-refutation. If logical laws exist, they must have something to do with the actual occurrence of belief as a psychological event.

So we might state the argument from logical laws as follows:

1. If naturalism is true, then logical laws either do not exist or are irrelevant to the formation of beliefs.

2. But logical laws are relevant to the formation of beliefs. (Implied by the existence of rational inference.)

3. Therefore, naturalism is false.

THE ARGUMENT FROM THE UNITY OF CONSCIOUSNESS IN RATIONAL INFERENCE

If one infers P from Q, then I take it that this involves a complex awareness in which one is aware of P, aware of Q, aware of the logical relation between P and Q, and on that account draws the conclusion that since Q is true, then P must be also. But what part of the person does this? The brain? The whole brain? Some part of the brain? If physicalism is true, then each of these moments of awareness is a different brain process. But what ties them all together in an inference? They all occur in the same bundle of neural states we call a brain, but so what? If each member of my philosophy class knows the correct answer to one question on the test, it is not the case on that account that the whole class knows the whole test. They could, on that account, still be flunking. It makes no sense to "parcel out" a complex awareness to parts that lack a comprehensive awareness.[11]

It can be objected, however, that this example of a whole class knowing all the answers is flawed because the whole class might work together to produce a test with all the answers even if no individual in the class knows them all, and that this is what materialists should and do say about the brain. But I am not talking about producing the inputs and outputs of rational awareness, I am talking about an occurrent (not dispositionally analyzable), simultaneous awareness of the contents of the premises, the acceptance of the truth of the premises, the perception of a relation of logical necessity between the premises and the conclusion, and the acceptance of the conclusion. This seems to require that something is aware of the premises, the conclusion and the logical relationship between them. By this I mean something that constitutes a metaphysical unit, not merely a functional unit deemed a "system" by an arbitrary act of the mind. After all, it is the mind that is being explained here. If the computer makes a correct inference, it is not a correct inference in the computer's perception, but in ours. As Stewart Goetz argues:

> The way we seem to ourselves manifests itself not only in language but also in what is known as "the binding problem" . . . which informs us that different soulish capacities (memory, decision, thought, and pain) are localized on different places in the brain. If we were to go on the ba-

---

[11]This argument is defended in Hasker, *Emergent Self*, pp. 123-35.

sis of this data alone, however, we would conclude that one part of the brain remembers, another decides, yet another philosophizes, and still another experiences pain. But this is not what we experience from a first-person point of view. I, a single and unified self, remember, decide, philosophize, and experience pain. And I am aware of doing all of this at the same time. Given that this is the way things seem to be, neuroscientists undertake to discover a single spot where the brain binds together all of the soulish events into a unified whole. What is important to recognize is that neuroscientists would not seek to find this spot, if it were not for our Augustinian first-person experience of ourselves.[12]

So we can state the argument from the unity of consciousness as follows:

1. If naturalism is true, then there is no single metaphysically unified entity that accepts the premises, perceives the logical connection between them and draws the conclusion.

2. But there is a single metaphysically unified entity that accepts the premises, perceives the logical connection between them and draws the conclusion. (Implied by the existence of rational inference.)

3. Therefore, naturalism is false.

THE ARGUMENT FROM THE RELIABILITY OF OUR RATIONAL FACULTIES

Still another argument can be given in terms of the reliability of our faculty of reasoning to give us truth. This is an argument made famous by Alvin Plantinga in *Warrant and Proper Function.*[13] The idea is this: If naturalism is true, then our faculties are, like everything else, the result of naturalistic evolution. But would naturalistic evolution give us mostly true beliefs, or merely just those falsehoods that are useful for

---

[12]Stewart Goetz, review of *Whatever Happened to the Soul*, by Nancey Murphy et al., *Philosophia Christi* 1, no. 2 (1999): 127.
[13]Alvin Plantinga, *Warrant and Proper Function* (Ithaca, N.Y.: Cornell University Press, 1993).

survival? In *The Last Word*, Thomas Nagel worries that a naturalistic view of the world would not adequately support our trust in our reasoning about the "nonapparent character of the world." By the nonapparent character of the world, I mean the aspects of reality that are not ordinarily observable by human beings. We could effectively go through our daily life without knowing, or needing to know, that physical reality has a molecular and an atomic structure. Natural selection would favor the development of reliable cognitive and rational abilities only insofar as those aptitudes helped protohumans cope with the challenges of their environment, but there is no reason to believe that we should trust our reasoning abilities beyond that original "coping" function. Hence a naturalistic evolutionary account of human beings would undermine the very confidence that naturalists must place in our ability to get to know the world through mathematical and scientific means.[14] The argument might be presented as follows:

1. If naturalism is true, then we should expect our faculties not to be reliable indicators of the nonapparent character of the world.

2. But our faculties do reliably reveal the nonapparent character of the world. (Presupposition of rational inference.)

3. Therefore, naturalism is false.

Thus, there are seven ways in which the argument from reason can be developed. These are seven phenomena that a naturalist cannot deny without denying the possibility of science itself. These phenomena seem on the face of things not to lend themselves to naturalistic analysis. The next stage in analyzing these arguments is to show that indeed these phenomena require explanatory dualism, which will be addressed in the next chapter.

---

[14]Thomas Nagel, *The Last Word* (New York: Oxford University Press, 1997), pp. 127-43. A Christian response to Nagel's fascinating book can be found in Douglas Groothuis, "Thomas Nagel's 'Last Word' on the Metaphysics of Rationality and Morality," *Philosophia Christi* 1, no. 1 (1999): 115-20.

FIVE

Explanatory Dualism

THE ARGUMENTS FROM REASON BEGIN with the insistence that certain things must be true of us as human beings in order to ensure the soundness of the kinds of claims we make on behalf of our reasoning. Our thoughts and words must be about other things. It must be possible that they be true or false. Our thoughts must not only be causally efficacious, but those thoughts must be efficacious in virtue of the content of those thoughts. There must be logical laws, and it must be possible for human beings to form beliefs because those beliefs follow logically from other beliefs. There must be a metaphysically unified center of consciousness that unifies the thought of the premises, the perception of the logical relationship between the premises and the conclusion, and the drawing of the conclusion. Our faculties must be reliable indicators not merely of what will be conducive to survival, but of what is true. These realities cannot be eliminated without undermining the process of rational inference, which in turn underlies the enterprise of doing science, as well as the enterprise of rational philosophical discourse. Since naturalistic philosophers invariably engage in rational inferences (for example, in arguments against theism from evil, or arguments against dualism based on Ockham's razor) and presuppose that science and mathematics are rational enterprises, they cannot deny these realities that I have mentioned without undermining the very enterprises that underlie their own position.

As I have indicated, the next step in the argument is to show that explanatory dualism is true, given the existence of these realities. By this I mean that while some events in nature can be explained in terms of purely mechanistic causes, the elements of rational inference that we discussed in the last chapter cannot. If certain states of the person are about others, if they can be true or false, if they can cause one another in virtue of their content, if there are logical laws and those logical laws can be relevant to the actual occurrence of belief as a psychological event, if there must be a metaphysical unity of consciousness underlying rational inference, and if our inferential faculties must be reliable, then human beings possess rational powers that are impossible for beings whose actions are governed entirely by the laws of physics.

On the other hand, if theism is true, then some events can occur that are not simply the results of chance and necessity. Consider the biblical monotheistic account of God's creating the world. Creation is neither a result of the mindless operation of natural laws, nor is it random. Monotheists in the biblical traditions believe the world was created because God thought it was good to create. Of course, this kind of explanatory dualism can also be supported by examples that are not specifically theistic. For example, if in the final analysis my left arm moves because I perform an act of will to cause it to move, and that act of will is free in the libertarian sense, then my desire to move it is a basic explanation of my arm's movement, not open to further reductive analysis.

Consistent naturalists, I maintain, must hold that in the final analysis, events take place by natural necessity and pure chance. In natural necessity, there is a physical state of the universe and the laws of physics, and these together yield a unique outcome. The outcome, however, is not chosen by anyone; it is simply what has to be. With the advent of quantum mechanics, however, physics has countenanced the possibility of uncaused events at the subatomic level. But this is pure chance and nothing more. In neither case is any event thought to occur for teleological reasons. The fact that one statement entails another statement seemingly must be irrelevant to how events are caused in the physical world.

Of course, sometimes naturalists advert to the existence of computers to resolve this difficulty and to demonstrate the compatibility of mechanism and purpose. And it is true that computers are undeniably physical systems operating under physical law. But in the case of computers, the compatibility between their mechanism and purpose is the result of mental states in the background that deliberately create this compatibility. Thus, the chess computer Deep Blue defeated world champion Garry Kasparov in their 1997 chess match. But Deep Blue's ability to defeat Kasparov was not the exclusive result of physical causation, unless the people on the programming team (such as Grandmaster Joel Benjamin) are entirely the result of physical causation. And that precisely is the point at issue between naturalists on the one hand and advocates of the argument from reason on the other. As Hasker points out:

> Computers function as they do because human beings have constructed them endowed with rational insight. A computer, in other words, is merely an extension of the rationality of its designers and users; it is no more an independent source of rational thought than a television set is an independent source of news and entertainment.[1]

INTENTIONALITY AND THE EFFICACY OF MENTAL STATES

Another response that is frequently given to the arguments from reason is the fact that evolution would, of course, select for rationality as opposed to irrationality. So therefore we should not be surprised if our reasoning capabilities are good at getting us the truth, since if they were not very good, our ancestors would have died without passing on their genes, and we wouldn't be here.

However, Hasker reminds us of what the real commitments of physicalism are:

---

[1] William Hasker, *Metaphysics* (Downers Grove, Ill.: InterVarsity Press, 1983), p. 49.

Certain complex assemblages of organic chemicals develop a kind of dynamic stability in their interactions with the environment, together with a capacity for self-replications, which leads us to say that they are alive. A variety of random physical forces lead to variations in the self-replicating assemblages, and some of the assemblages are more successful than others in maintaining and reproducing themselves. Over time, some of these assemblages become more complex than the earliest forms by several orders of magnitude, and their behaviors and interactions with the surrounding environment also become more complex. Nevertheless, the entire process is governed by, and explicable in terms of, the ordinary laws of physics and chemistry. Put differently, it is never necessary to go outside of the physical configurations and physical laws in order to predict the future behavior of these assemblages; this is the "closure of the physical."[2]

The problem is this: If the physical realm is causally closed, then it looks on the face of things as if it will go on its merry way regardless of what mental states exist, and if this is the case, then mental states simply do not matter with respect to what events are caused in the physical world.

The Darwinian argument, if it works at all, would show, if there were mental states and if those mental states could be causally effective in virtue of their content, how sound strategies would prevail over unsound strategies. However, it is my contention that a consistent physicalism leads to the conclusion that there are no mental states with propositional content, and if such states were to exist they would be epiphenomenal, that is, without any causal efficacy. What is more, there is certainly the possibility that what is conducive to discovering the truth might not be conducive to survival and vice versa. We might survive better not by knowing the truth but by believing just those falsehoods that would be most conducive to survival.

It might be thought that intentionality or "about-ness" is simply

---

[2]William Hasker, *The Emergent Self* (Ithaca, N.Y.: Cornell University Press, 1999), p. 77.

another word for reference and that we do have causal theories of reference that are supposed to do the job of accounting for reference. Such theories explain how it is possible for one word or one thought to be about something else in virtue of the causal relationships in which it stands to the object being referred to. But, for example, Saul Kripke's theory of reference is a theory about how reference is *transmitted*; what accounts for the naming of something in the first place is, for Kripke, a naming ceremony.[3] However, a naming ceremony is itself an intentional act. There have been attempts to provide a physicalistically acceptable account of how such naming ceremonies are possible, but these attempts, so far as I have been able to tell, have been unsuccessful.[4] According to Geoffrey Madell,

> Reflection and experience of having a thought ought to lead us to say that the thought's being about something is an intrinsic and nondispositional property of the act of consciousness. My thinking idly about dear old Uncle George is an event in consciousness, and the thought I have has an object such that its having that object is an actual or categorical property of the event in consciousness which is the occurrent thought. What is more, it is quite unclear what an *analysis* of a thought's directedness could possibly amount to. The directedness, or "about-ness" of the thought is a basic fact of experience, and there appears nothing to which it could possibly be reduced in analysis. If we are to pay attention to the phenomenology of experience, these two factors, the nondispositionality and the irreducibility of the directedness of thought, seem absolutely undeniable.[5]

Nevertheless, these "facts" of experience seem clearly to be not acceptable from the materialist point of view, and so materialists have

---

[3]Saul Kripke, *Naming and Necessity* (Cambridge, Mass.: Harvard University Press, 1982).
[4]M. Rice, "Why Devitt Can't Name His Cat," *Southern Journal of Philosophy* 27, no. 2 (1989): 273-84.
[5]Geoffrey Madell, *Mind and Materialism* (Edinburgh: Edinburgh University Press, 1988), p. 11.

invariably attempted to provide a *dispositional* account of what it is for a thought to be about something else. Some terms in our vocabulary seem to be the sorts of terms that lend themselves to dispositional analysis. That is, the term can be explicated in terms of the tendency on the part of the thing the term denotes to behave in certain ways. A bottle is brittle only in the case that it breaks easily upon impact. But it seems to be absurd to apply this kind of analysis to the claim that a particular thought is about something else. Consider the following two scenarios.

1. I sit in a chair, have an idle thought about my cousin Warren, forget the thought completely and go on with my day.

2. I sit in a chair, have an idle thought about my cousin Don, forget the thought completely and go on with my day.

In these two scenarios my thoughts are about different people, yet they produce precisely the same effects, namely, none. I know whom I am thinking about when I have the thought, though it causes no effects in my behavior. The difference is simply a difference in my first-person world; it cannot be accounted for from the outside. Looking at the world materialistically, operating from a third-person perspective that, as Lewis puts it, looks *at* rather than *along* my thought process, will never capture what my thoughts are about.[6]

But suppose, contrary to what I have suggested, a materialist philosophy can account for the fact that one thought can be about something else. There are still difficulties here concerning how one thought can cause another thought in virtue of its content. Hasker argues that if materialism is true, even if one mental event can cause another event, the fact that such an event has a mental description will be irrelevant to the causal relationships it enters into. Materialism maintains that causal relationships are governed

---

[6]C. S. Lewis, "Meditation on a Toolshed," in *God in the Dock* (Grand Rapids, Mich.: Eerdmans, 1970), pp. 212-15.

by physical laws, not by mental content and not by logical laws.[7]

In defending the claim that mental descriptions are causally irrelevant if physicalism is true against the possibility of genuine mental causation for the materialist, Hasker argues that we can surely imagine a possible world in which the physical is the same as it is in the actual world, but in which there are no mental states whatsoever. In that world "people" are not people after all, but merely zombies. If events occur in the world in virtue of physical causation only and there is no other kind of causation in existence, then the entire mental state of everything in the world is simply irrelevant. To back up this claim, he offers a possible-worlds analysis of counterfactual claims:

a. She would have accepted the belief if she had not seen that it was supported by good reasons.

b. She would not have accepted the belief if she had not seen that it was supported by good reasons.

According to a possible-worlds analysis of a counterfactual claim, a counterfactual is true if the consequent is true in the possible world most similar to this one in which the antecedent is true. For example, if we are analyzing the truth of the conditional "if Al Gore had won in Florida, then he would now be president," we must imagine a possible world that is as similar to this one as possible but in which Gore won in Florida, and ask ourselves if, in that world, Gore would now be president. If the answer is *yes*, then the counterfactual is true, but if the answer is *no*, then the counterfactual is false.

Hasker claims that if we are analyzing the consequences of physicalism, we have to look at a world physically identical to the actual world, that is, a possible world that is identical to this one at the physical level but in which the laws connecting mental states to physical

---

[7]Hasker, *Emergent Self*, pp. 64-75.

states do not pertain. In such a world everything would be physically just like the world we live in, but the persons would be zombies, devoid of conscious experience, beings whose states have no propositional content. That is, their thoughts are not about anything. If we examine such a world, we have to say that the counterfactuals that must be true in order for rational inference to be possible would have to be regarded as false.[8]

Terence Horgan, on the other hand, argues that counterfactuals such as these are true on materialist assumptions. In so doing he claims that when one considers possible worlds one must restrict oneself to "pertinently similar worlds," (PSWs hereafter), and although he does not mention Hasker's zombie world, he does seem to suggest that such a world would fall outside the class of PSWs and therefore not be relevant for consideration. As he puts it in another context, "Weird worlds are not PSWs."[9]

Perhaps the argument might be developed further along these lines: We know from science that you can look at the same phenomena on different levels. We can perhaps imagine a world in which the physical state is the same but the chemical state is different, but we are inclined to suppose that the chemical is simply the physical "writ large," and that something with the same physical structure as water would have to in fact be water. In the case of biological states, again, we can talk about the possibility of a world with the same physical state as this one in which, say, there are no digestive systems, but in fact that too seems rather implausible, even if there is no clear reduction of biological states to physical states. So what about a world like this one but with no mental states? Isn't that equally implausible and weird?

---

[8] Ibid.
[9] Terence Horgan, "Mental Quasation," in *Philosophical Perspectives*, vol. 3, *Philosophy of Mind and Action Theory*, ed. James E. Tomberlin (Atascadero, Calif.: Ridgeview, 1991), p. 64.

But in the cases of chemistry and biology it is easy to see how those upper-level states must be the way they are given the state of the physical. In the case of mental states, however, the supervenience, if it obtains at all, stands in need of explanation. Why are people in such-and-such a mental state if and only if their brains are in such-and-such a state? If we can assume that physicalism is true from the outset, and we believe that there is rational inference, then of course there has to be a reconciliation of these two great facts out there somewhere, but on pain of begging the question, one cannot simply presume that physicalism is true. Besides, the mental, insofar as it is involved in rational inference, obeys a radically different set of laws from the laws of physics, namely, the laws of logic. The laws of logic do not result from the laws governing the physical order; in fact, they are supposed to apply not only to this world, with its physical characteristics, but to all possible worlds.

LAWS OF LOGIC

Laws of logic and their role in human thought provide another line of argument for explanatory dualism. Unless the laws of logic can figure in basic explanations, then in the last analysis we never do believe Q because we believe P, believe Q, and believe that P entails Q. Lewis uses the expression "an act of knowing is determined by what it knows."[10] If the cat is on the mat, the fact that the cat is on the mat generates a causal chain through my perceptual apparatus that provides me with the knowledge that the cat is on the mat. If these perceptual processes are purely physical processes, then perhaps we can account for this without rejecting physicalism. But what if what we know is that if P entails Q, then Q must also be true? What reality causes us to believe that? How can it be true in this kind of a case that

---

[10]C. S. Lewis, *Miracles: A Preliminary Study* (New York: Macmillan Paperbacks Edition, 1978), p. 17.

one thought causes another thought not by actually being its ground, but by being seen to be the ground for it? If physicalism is true, then all the causal chains that exist connect particular states in the physical, spatio-temporal world with one another. How could there possibly be states of something that not only do not exist in any particular place or time, but are true in all possible worlds?

A. J. Ayer, in the tradition of empiricism, argued that our knowledge of logical truths is knowledge of how our ideas are related to one another, and that such knowledge does not give us knowledge of the world. According to Ayer, if we assume that our knowledge of necessary truths is about the world, then

> we shall be obliged to admit that there are some truths about the world which we can know independently of experience; even though we cannot conceivably observe that all objects have them. And we shall have to accept it as a mysterious inexplicable fact that our thought has this power to reveal to us authoritatively the nature of objects that we have never observed.[11]

In other words, Ayer maintains that if our knowledge of necessary truths is really about the world, then it would be an inexplicable mystery. But if it is simply about how our ideas are related to one another, then it isn't mysterious at all. All our knowledge of the world, according to Ayer, will be based on experience, and he does not perceive such knowledge as mysterious.

Robert M. Adams, however, argues that restricting our knowledge of necessary truths to "relations of ideas" does not in fact render such knowledge free of mystery.

> For if necessary truths reveal features or relations of thoughts, they reveal features or relations of thought that we have not yet thought, as well as those that we have thought. If I know that *modus ponens* is a

---

[11] A. J. Ayer, *Language, Truth and Logic,* 2nd ed. (1936; New York: Dover, n.d.), p. 73.

valid argument form, I know that it will be valid for thoughts that I think tomorrow as well as for thoughts that I have thought today. If this is a knowledge of properties and relations of the thoughts involved, then the question how I can know properties and relations of thoughts I have not yet experienced seems as pressing as the question of how I could know properties and objects outside my mind that I have not experienced. The retreat to abstract or mental objects does not help to explain what we want explained.[12]

In short, Ayer's own view requires that we know something about thoughts that we have not yet thought, and that is just as naturalistically mysterious as the idea that we know objects outside the mind that we have not yet experienced.

Adams claims that in fact we cannot escape the conclusion that we know certain things about our future thoughts. These things are not learned from experience, and therefore it is reasonable to suppose that we have a faculty for knowing such truths nonempirically. He considers the possibility that a theory of natural selection might provide a naturalistic explanation for our possession of such a faculty, but he maintains that this explanation is not fully satisfactory:

> But there are aspects of our knowledge of necessary truths for which this evolutionary explanation is less than satisfying. That is particularly true of the knowledge of modality which most concerns us in this discussion. During formative periods of human evolution, what survival value was there in recognizing necessary truths as necessary? Very little, I should think. Logical or absolute necessity as such as a philosophoumenon [i.e., a philosophical phenomenon] which would hardly have helped the primitive hunter or gatherer in finding food or shelter, nor does it seem in any way important to the building of a viable primitive society. Those of us who think we have some faculty for recognizing truth on many of the issues discussed in this paper can hardly

---

[12]Robert M. Adams, "Divine Necessity," in *The Virtue of Faith and Other Essays in Philosophical Theology* (New York: Oxford University Press, 1987), p. 216.

believe that such a faculty was of much use to our evolving ancestors;
nor is there any obvious way in which such a faculty, and its reliability,
are inevitable by-products of faculties that did have survival value.[13]

But there seems to me to be a further difficulty with this kind of
evolutionary response. The mere presence of survival value does not
guarantee that we really have a naturalistic explanation on our
hands. The item possessing the survival value must be physically re-
alizable. Suppose two desert tribes, the Yahvites and the Baalites, are
competing for scarce resources in the desert. The Yahvites receive
periodic manna from heaven and survive, passing on their genes.
The Baalites, on the other hand, die out, because they receive no
manna from heaven. Now the fact that the ability to receive manna
from heaven has survival value does not mean that the explanation
of their survival is naturalistic. Because objects involved in the Yahvites' survival are supernatural, the explanation is not naturalistic
even though it is, in some sense, evolutionary.

Adams considers the possibility that human minds simply, by nature, have the capacity to recognize necessary truths as necessary. He
maintains that

> we are too easily mistaken about necessary truths and too often unable
> to recognize them. And there is too much reason to believe that other
> mechanisms or causal processes are involved in our knowing them.
> But I seriously entertain the hypotheses that there is a mind to which
> nature it simply belongs to be able to recognize necessary truths. In-
> deed I am inclined to believe that such a mind belongs to God.[14]

He claims that this provides an argument for the existence of God,
not a demonstration, but a "theoretical advantage" of theism that al-
lows us to explain something that would otherwise be difficult to explain. He continues:

---

[13]Ibid., p. 217.
[14]Ibid., pp. 217-18.

And that opens the way for another explanation of our knowledge of necessary truths: an explanation in terms of divine illumination. Suppose that necessary truths do determine and explain facts about the real world. If God of his very nature knows the necessary truths, and if he has created us, he could have constructed us in such a way that we would at least commonly recognize necessary truths as necessary. In this way there would be a causal connection between what is necessarily true about real objects and our believing it to be necessarily true about them. It would not be an incredible accident or an inexplicable mystery that our beliefs agreed with the objects in this.[15]

THE RELIABILITY OF OUR RATIONAL FACULTIES

Another version of the argument regarding explanatory dualism concerns the reliability of our rational faculties. In chapter thirteen of *Miracles*, Lewis develops a version of the argument from reason based on our probability judgments. Responding to Hume's famous "Of Miracles," Lewis raises the point that Hume himself made in his discussion of the claim that the future will resemble the past, namely, that our probability judgments depend on some form of the principle of the uniformity of nature being true. Hume claimed that we cannot argue for the principle of the uniformity of nature based on experience that the future will resemble the past, because any extrapolation of past experience to the future will invariably appeal to the resemblance principle being defended. So, Lewis asks, why should we accept the resemblance principle? He mentions two reasons given by Hume: first, that we can't help accepting it, and second, that in planning our lives, we must, for practical reasons, leave out of account the possibility that nature will not behave as we expect it to. But, Lewis says, if the causes of a belief are nonrational, then they could lead us just as easily to a false belief as to a true belief. But, he says, there is a third basis for this belief basis for the be-

---

lief in the principle of the uniformity of nature, the idea that we are influenced by "an innate sense of the fitness of things." However, if naturalism is true, then that "innate sense" is just a byproduct of evolution designed to help us survive, not to find the truth. If theism is true, then "our repugnance to disorder is derived from nature's creator and ours." In fact, Lewis, following Whitehead, suggests that the scientific enterprise historically arose because the theistic beliefs of the early scientists led them to expect a systematic order in the universe. As he puts it, "Men became scientific because they expected Law in Nature, and they expected Law in Nature because they believed in a Legislator."[16]

Arthur James Balfour, the British Prime Minister-philosopher, in his book *Theism and Humanism* (a book that Lewis greatly admired), argued that with respect to our belief in an objective, independent external world, several scientific convictions have contributed to the success of the scientific enterprise. But those convictions were not, in the first instance, based on experimental evidence; they are rather preinvestigatory convictions that proved to be fruitful. Among these are

1. our belief in an objective, independently existing external world (and this in spite of the lengthy process of mediation between the world and ourselves that the science of perception describes);

2. the uniformity of nature and governance by the laws of nature;

3. an intuitive, nonmathematical conception of probability, which is immeasurably helpful in coming to an understanding of our world (today Balfour would make his point by pointing to the manifest failure of frequency theories of prior probabilities);

4. our belief in the conservation of matter and energy; and

5. our belief that the world must have an atomic structure.

---

[16]Lewis, *Miracles*, p. 106.

These scientific convictions, Balfour maintained, are not based on the physical evidence. Rather, they are the outworking of convictions that scientists brought to their investigation of the natural world. If all of this is just the product of naturalistic evolution, then why are we so sure, and why have we always been so sure, that the world "out there" corresponds to these convictions? We don't have a solid basis purely on naturalistic evolution. On the other hand, if theism is true, then these beliefs make a good deal more sense. Belief in the reliability of our belief-producing mechanisms makes sense on theistic assumptions, but not on naturalistic assumptions.[17]

With respect to the argument from the reliability of our rational faculties, Theodore Drange suggests that generally applicable faculty for knowing the truth about the world would be of survival value and therefore be selected for by natural selection, even though its applicability goes far beyond what might be useful for survival in the particular environment (in our case humans in the hunter-gatherer stage).[18] But I think that such a claim is by no means obviously correct. Of course some creatures are able to survive and procreate without any beliefs whatsoever. What is required for survival is effective response to the environment, not accurate knowledge of that environment. So perhaps evolution could select for something that wasn't so accurate in depicting the environment but provided a more efficient way of getting the biologically correct response to the envi-

---

[17]Arthur James Balfour, *Theism and Humanism* (New York: Hodder & Stoughton, 1915), pp. 149-268. Various sources on Lewis credit Balfour with having provided the foundation for Lewis's case against naturalism. To the best of my knowledge, however, the connection between Balfour and Lewis went unnoticed in Lewis scholarship until my dissertation advisor, Hugh Chandler, noticed a similarity between a Balfour argument criticized by G. E. Moore in an early essay and Lewis's argument against naturalism. In fact, Chandler thought that Moore's criticism of Balfour and Anscombe's criticism of Lewis were similar. Shortly thereafter I sent a letter pointing out the similarities to the Bulletin of the New York C. S. Lewis Society, and other commentators have picked up on the relationship since.
[18]Theodore Drange, "Reply to Reppert," *Philosophia Christi* 5 (fall-winter 2003).

ronment. If the chief enemy of a creature is a foot-long snake, perhaps some inner programming to attack everything a foot long would be more effective from the point of view of survival than the complicated ability to distinguish reptiles from mammals or amphibians. The more complex our knowledge abilities are, the larger a brain will be required to house these faculties. As a result, creatures with large brains will have a longer period of immaturity and vulnerability, and more things can go wrong before their genes can be passed along. It is far from clear that a general ability to learn what is true will be helpful from an evolutionary standpoint, and there are good prima facie reasons to accept Alvin Plantinga's assessment that if naturalism is true, then the probability that our faculties will be reliable is low at worst and inscrutable at best.[19] This assessment contrasts unfavorably with the situation given theism. If we are the creations of a good God interested in our epistemic well-being, then we should expect to have epistemic faculties that are reliable.[20]

A DUALISM OF FUNDAMENTAL EXPLANATIONS

All of these lines of argument support the idea of a dualism of fundamental explanations, that is, the idea that we cannot expunge purposes from the basic level of explanation without radically undermining the very scientific enterprise that provides the primary foundation for philosophical naturalism. There are, in this area, a number of "theoretical advantages" for a theistic account of the world over a naturalistic one that can be found when we reflect carefully on how we know that world.

Of course, it might be argued that explanatory dualism, as I am understanding it, can be handled metaphysically by accepting a property

---

[19]Plantinga's best treatment of what he calls the evolutionary argument against naturalism is found in Alvin Plantinga, *Warranted Christian Belief* (New York: Oxford University Press, 2000), pp. 227-40.
[20]The argument in this paragraph was suggested to me by Dennis Monokroussos.

dualism as opposed to substance dualism, and that a theistic framework is not needed to support explanatory dualism. If by dualism you
mean the Cartesian conception of a soul that does not have a spatial
location, the argument for explanatory dualism does not require that
souls not be in space. Jaegwon Kim considers the possibility that there
are souls located in space. But concerning such souls, he raises the
question of whether or not they have the same kind of "impenetrability" as we find in physical objects: just as not more than one physical
object can occupy the same area of space, can no more than one soul
occupy any spatial point? If they do have this same kind of "impenetrability" (and it does seem to be part of what's involved when you say
something occupies an area of space), he asks, "Why aren't souls just
material objects, albeit of a special, and strange, kind?"[21] If such things
are not constrained by the laws of physics in the way that ordinary material objects are, I would call such things souls rather than material
objects. You may call them material objects if you wish. Of course, my
argument doesn't require that souls be spatial, it is neutral whether or
not they are spatial. As Lewis puts it,

> To call the act of knowing—the act, not of remembering that something
> was so in the past, but of "seeing" that it must be so always and in any
> possible world—to call this act "supernatural," does some violence to
> our ordinary linguistic usage. But of course we don't mean by this that it
> is spooky, or sensational, or even (in any religious sense) "spiritual." We
> mean only that it "won't fit in"; that such an act, to be what it claims to
> be—and if it is not, all our thinking is discredited—cannot be merely the
> exhibition at a particular place and time of that total, and largely mind-
> less, system of events we call "Nature." It must break sufficiently free
> from that universal chain in order to be determined by what it knows.[22]

In fact, Lewis deliberately avoids using terms such as *souls* or *spir-*

[21] Jaegwon Kim, "Lonely Souls," in *Soul, Body and Survival*, ed. Kevin Corcoran (Ithaca,
N.Y.: Cornell University Press, 2001), p. 42.
[22] Lewis, *Miracles*, p. 23.

its in the development of his argument. I have identified my position as dualist because the argument does point to a dualism of fundamental explanations and fundamental laws. As such, my argument puts me in conflict with materialism as commonly understood by most contemporary materialists. If someone wants to argue that it nonetheless accords with some form of mind-body materialism, that's fine with me. They should just expect to be written out of the materialist camp by the likes of Daniel Dennett.

Perhaps, however, theism is not necessary to account for reasoning as we know and understand it. I would agree with that claim. Lewis himself, when he was persuaded by the argument, accepted not theism (and certainly not Christianity) but rather absolute idealism. Idealism and pantheism do not have the problem of claiming that nonrational processes are fundamental and then having to wonder how rational processes could emerge from these. So the arguments from reason are not arguments for accepting theism as opposed to idealism or pantheism. Indeed, we find Lewis making independent arguments against these positions.

It should be noted, though, for many people today, the live options are some form of traditional theism on the one hand and some form of naturalistic atheism on the other. The arguments from reason, if successful, give a person for whom these are the live options a reason to select theism and to reject naturalism. There may, however, be other live options for some, and the arguments from reason may or may not be arguments against those positions.

Perhaps all we need in order for reason to exist, however, is an "emergent" mind, one that is generated by the material processes of the universe. Hasker argues against the view that God directly created human souls, and maintains instead that matter has the potentiality to produce the soul.[23] Nevertheless, the argument here does

---

[23]Hasker, *Emergent Self*, pp. 147-97.

not need to take a stand on whether God creates each and every soul. We still must ask how it came to be that matter had such characteristics. *Why* does matter have that capability, if it is simply part of a mindless universe? But if God creates matter, then its having those capabilities might at least possibly make sense.

Lewis considers the possibility that a cosmic mind could emerge from matter (a doctrine familiar in his day as emergent evolution), but he says that if such a cosmic mind were the product of mindless nature, then we would have no more reason to trust it than we would have to trust a physical mind.

> The cosmic mind will only help us if we put it at the beginning, if we suppose it to be, not the product of the total system, but the basic, original, self-existent Fact which exists in its own right. But to admit that sort of a cosmic mind is to admit a God outside nature, a transcendent and supernatural God.[24]

In short, the force of the arguments from reason is to show that the fundamental fact of the universe must be rational. Theism is a worldview that fits this requirement, though I have not attempted to show that it is the only one that does. Naturalism, theism's chief rival for the mind of the West, does not.

---

[24]Lewis, *Miracles*, p. 30.

The Inadequacy Objection

IN DEVELOPING LEWIS'S ARGUMENT in the previous three chapters, I have considered some arguments against the arguments from reason. I have considered the objections posed by Anscombe, in particular her claim that reasons-explanations are not causal explanations and therefore cannot compete with causal explanations. I have also discussed the objection that physical and rational explanations must be compatible because computers are both mechanistic and rational. I have also considered the argument that since evolution would certainly select for sound reasoning over unsound reasoning, there is no problem in accounting for rationality in a mechanistic, Darwinian world.

But some objections require further consideration. If the arguments from reason are good arguments, we might want to ask why more philosophers do not defend them. Of course, some do defend them, but they are surely not among the most discussed of theistic arguments, and physicalism remains the prevailing paradigm in the philosophy of mind. I do not believe that this is because physicalists actually think they have a well-developed account of how reason is possible in a naturalistic world. Many naturalistic philosophers, in fact, are perfectly willing to admit that there is a great difficulty in coming up with such an explanation. Book after book is written to attempt to resolve this puzzle, and some naturalist philosophers freely use the term "mystery" in speaking about the mind. I believe that philosophers reject the arguments from reason because of a prevailing conviction that when the best naturalistic resources available are

employed to produce an understanding of the world and mysteries
are left over, we do little or nothing to explain those mysteries by in-
voking "souls" or by explaining them in terms of God. Following
Theodore Drange, I will call this objection the inadequacy objection
and will discuss it in this chapter.[1]

Keith Parsons puts the objection as follows:

> Creationist "explanations" do not explain. When we appeal to the in-
> scrutable acts and incomprehensible powers of an occult being to ac-
> count for mysterious phenomena, we only deepen the mystery. Like
> Nagel (pp. 132-33), I regard such "explanations" as mere markers for
> our ignorance, placeholders for explanations we hope someday to get.[2]

And in a subsequent response to my version of the argument, Parsons
says:

> Reppert charges that I have question-beggingly assumed that physical
> explanation is the only legitimate kind, and that this biases my whole
> argument. Not so. My objection to supernaturalism is not that it fails
> to conform to an arbitrary ideal of mechanical explanation. I contrast
> physical explanations with supernatural "explanations" because I
> honestly cannot see that the latter explain at all. Explanations should
> enhance understanding. What is it to "understand" a phenomenon?
> Karel Lambert and Gordon Brittan suggest that scientific understand-
> ing of a particular topic of concern occurs when an explanation shows
> or exhibits a new piece of information and serves one or more of the
> following functions:
>
> 1. It tells why the topic of concern was to be expected (i.e., it provides
>   a universal or statistical law that covers the topic of concern).

---

[1] Theodore M. Drange, "'First Rebuttal' in the Drange-Wilson Debate," The Secular
Web, Modern Library (1999) <http://www.infidels.org/library/modern/theodore_drange/
drange-wilson/drange2.html>.

[2] Keith M. Parsons, "Defending Objectivity," *Philo* 2 (spring-summer 1999): 84; Thomas
Nagel, *The Last Word* (Oxford: Oxford University Press, 1997), pp. 132-33.

2. It tells how the topic of concern was brought about (i.e. what caused it).

3. It tells why the topic of concern was to be favored instead of a contrasting state of affairs.

However, postulating nonphysical souls (or God) does not accomplish any of these goals. We have no "laws of supernature," and hence cannot predict instances of consciousness. We have no causal mechanism to explain how souls accomplish their alleged effects, and postulating souls gives us no reason to expect conscious humans instead of, say, conscious snails.[3]

To answer this line of objection, we must first point out the considerable explanatory power of ordinary common sense, explanations that advert to purposes or advert to what thoughts are about, quite apart from any scientific reduction. If I know that Keith Parsons is an avid fan of the Georgia Bulldogs who despises the Florida Gators, I know that he will celebrate a Georgia victory over Florida and will be disappointed should there be a Gator triumph. I may not be able to express these claims in terms of strict laws, but I can form probabilistic expectations concerning what I expect Parsons to do. In fact, if someone were to provide me with a neurophysiological account of why Parsons is celebrating a Bulldog triumph, this would provide me far less understanding of his behavior than would a common sense, intentional explanation.

Now what does this all have to do with the question of souls? Well, given the fact that we do have a teleological explanation for a piece of human behavior, we can further ask whether or not this teleological explanation is an explanation at the most basic level of analysis. If physicalism is true, then there must be some further, mechanistic analysis that explains why a teleological explanation can be given. If dualism is

---

[3] Keith M. Parsons, "Further Reflections on the Argument from Reason," *Philo* 3 (spring-summer 2000): 95.

true, however, then the intentional explanation can be a basic explanation. Nevertheless, intentional explanations, with or without the possibility of further reduction, do allow us to form expectations as to what is and is not more likely to occur. Such teleological explanations do provide a cause for what happens, and only on the question-begging assumption that in the last analysis causal analyses cannot be teleological can it be said that a causal explanation has not been provided. Contrary to what Parsons says, nonreduced intentional explanations can satisfy Lambert and Brittan's criteria for explanation.

Explanations can be either basic or nonbasic. If the explanations are nonbasic, then the explanation can be explained further in terms of its constituent parts. If someone were to give me a sleeping pill, I might ask, "What is it about this pill that will put me to sleep?" Now it would not be appropriate for someone to answer by saying, "It's just the nature of that pill to put you to sleep. That's just what it does. It has a 'dormative virtue.'" I know, on the basis of my background knowledge, that pills have effects due to the chemical characteristics of their constituent parts. And this is a more basic explanation. But that chemical explanation is still not necessarily a truly basic explanation. However, when the explanation is basic, then we end up saying that it is the nature of something to have such-and-such a characteristic. A basic explanation would be to say that the properties of the basic elements of matter are the way they are because it is their nature to be that way. If something is composed of component parts, then it has the characteristics it does because of the characteristics of those component parts; if it has no component parts, then a reductive explanation cannot be given. A physicalist is not immune from giving basic explanations that appeal to the nature of things. He or she must provide them when they are pressed to answer, for example, the question of why the basic physical elements of the universe have the characteristics that they do.

We can call the soul "supernatural" and complain that we have no "laws of supernature," but we cannot pretend that we have no explanations. If the complaint is that we have no strict laws governing the activities of the soul, then we have to admit that in many cases our best science provides us with no strict laws. If we accept an indeterministic interpretation of quantum mechanics, then we have no strict laws in physics either. Yet if this means we have nothing by which to form probabilistic expectations, then it seems to me that the claim is patently false. Information about how Parsons tends to behave does give us expectations about how he will behave, and this will be true even if Parsons has a soul whose activities cannot be given a mechanistic explanation. These probabilistic explanations are indeed "laws of supernature"; the fact that they are not deterministic laws does not nullify the fact that they are indeed laws.

Parsons also argues that accepting the existence of a nonphysical soul that interacts causally with a body will result in our having to accept the existence of something that violates the first law of thermodynamics. Considering the dualism of William Hart, Parsons writes:

> Hart's light-soul proposal is unacceptable for at least two other reasons. First, on his hypothesis, electromagnetic energy is not conserved; it simply disappears from the physical universe, mysteriously converted to non-physical, "psychic energy." Presumably, when the interaction goes the other way, when souls affect physical bodies, the required energy just appears, literally, out of nowhere (by definition, the physical cannot be closed for substance dualists). In short, Hart postulates miraculous violations of the first law of thermodynamics, the law of conservation of energy. Hart's proposal is like the Sidney Harris cartoon, where a scientist has filled the board with mathematical scribbles, but his second step reads "And then a miracle occurs." Another scientist comments dryly, "I think you should be more explicit here in step two."[4]

---

[4]Ibid., p. 94.

However, as Lewis points out:

If laws of Nature are necessary truths, no miracles can break them, but then no miracle needs to break them. It is with them as the laws of arithmetic. If I put six pennies into a drawer on Monday and six more on Tuesday, the laws decree that—other things being equal—I shall find twelve pennies in there on Wednesday. But if the drawer had been robbed I may in fact find only two. Something will have been broken (the lock on the drawer or the laws of England) but the laws of arithmetic will not have been broken.[5]

The laws of nature, in short, tell you what will happen apart from any outside interference. Conservation laws apply on the assumption that nothing outside the natural system is interfering with it. Dualistic interactionism supposes that the physical is not closed, so it should not be surprising that, given dualistic interaction, the laws governing the physical order should not be comprehensive.

Parsons also raises the objection that on a dualist view of mind, which the argument seems to require, there is a serious problem as to how two distinct types of substances, such as the mind and the body, could possibly interact.[6] One cannot, he says, refute this objection by saying there is equally a mystery about how physical transactions occur. Science provides explanations as to how things interact, and science improves these explanations progressively.[7]

Now the claim that there is a mystery about how a soul can interact with a body is a familiar one. But without further explanation it seems open to Hasker's charge that "this argument may well hold the all-time record for overrated objections to philosophical positions."[8] First of all, Hume did show us that there is nothing we can find even in physical causal relationships, such as necessary connection,

[5]C. S. Lewis, *Miracles* (New York: Macmillan, 1960), p. 58.
[6]Parsons, "Further Reflections," p. 94.
[7]Ibid., p. 93.
[8]William Hasker, *The Emergent Self* (Ithaca, N.Y.: Cornell University Press, 1999), p. 150.

which could dispel the mystery of how A causes B. Second, this argument usually amounts to the question "by what mechanisms does the mind interact with the body?" Put thus, however, the argument begs the question, because it assumes that all causation is mechanistic. And that is precisely what is at issue here. Third, while the argument is designed to show that there is some aspect of the human person that has the essential capacity to perceive logical connections, that entity still could very well be spatially locatable.

But Parsons is right in supposing that a materialist view of the mind does render the mind amenable to certain types of scientific understanding in a way that a dualist view does not. But is tractability to be purchased at the cost of undermining the scientific enterprise itself? The argument from reason is designed to show that the scientific enterprise as we know it would not exist if a fully materialistic/naturalistic account of the scientific enterprise were true. Attempts to apply a materialist theory of mind to the process of science itself has led to a denial of the centrality of truth on the part of philosophers of science; Paul and Patricia Churchland are a case in point. Is it more dangerous to the scientific enterprise to suggest that a comprehensive "scientific" account of cognition cannot be correct, or to suggest that truth should not be the goal of our rational deliberations? Bertrand Russell, hardly an enemy of naturalism or a friend of Christian apologetics, wrote:

> A physicist looks for causes; that does not necessarily imply that there are causes everywhere. A man may look for gold without assuming that there is gold everywhere; if he finds gold, well and good, if he does not he's had bad luck. The same is true when physicists look for causes.[9]

---

[9]Bertrand Russell and F. C. Copleston, "The Existence of God—A Debate," in *A Modern Introduction to Philosophy*, ed. Paul Edwards and Arthur Pap, rev. ed. (New York: Free Press, 1965), p. 480.

It is sometimes suggested that widespread acceptance of the argument from reason would undermine the endeavor to understand the mind scientifically, a project that has resulted in significant results in cognitive science and artificial intelligence. However, nothing prevents science from investigating cognition to find whatever scientific explanations can be found. Is it necessary for the scientific enterprise to have a supreme faith in our ability to find naturalistic explanations? People who believe in a theistic God and people who do not even believe the physical world to be real can participate in the scientific enterprise. A more controversial suggestion would be that cognition might also be investigated scientifically from an intelligent design perspective. However successful or unsuccessful intelligent design investigations might be, I believe that they cannot be disqualified from science simply because they appeal to an intelligent designer.[10]

Mechanistic science is successful in many cases where the subject matter lends itself to a mechanistic approach. When it comes to such things as continental drift, we do not have much of any common sense understanding of why continents move the way they do, so we have to wait for science to give us the story. In the case of human behavior, we have a teleological account that we know by common sense in virtue of our being human beings. While science has supplemented common sense, it has not replaced it with scientific analysis. The question now arises as to whether these common sense accounts are basic explanations or whether they themselves have to be analyzed in terms of a more fundamental mechanistic substratum. It might be nice to explain all of this mechanistically, but not at the price of reducing to nonsense the very activity of rational inference on which science is based. One cannot perform scientific research with a fixed, preconceived idea of what the explanations will

---

[10]For a development of intelligent design theory, see William Dembski, *Intelligent Design* (Downers Grove, Ill.: InterVarsity Press, 1999).

be. If we did, we would not have accepted quantum indeterminism or a beginning of the universe at the big bang. The kind of explanation that worked for falling apples and drifting continents may not work for consciousness and reasoning.

OBJECTIONS TO EXPLANATORY DUALISM

Jaegwon Kim tries to put meat on the bones of the antidualist argument in another way. He asks what it is that connects a Cartesian soul with a particular body so as to enable causal connections between them. Some physical things can interact with other physical things, while others cannot interact with other physical things because of the presence or absence of a spatial relationship between them. (I couldn't have killed him; I was in New Mexico at the time and he was in Arizona.) But if, as the Cartesian tradition suggests, the soul is not spatial, how does the soul connect with my body as opposed to someone else's body?[11]

Now in this book I have not argued that there is a nonspatial soul. What I have tried to argue is that something must exist that is sufficiently free from the nexus of nonrational causation to be determined not by the positions of particles and the laws of physics but by the truth it knows, even if that truth is not local to any particular place or time. Kim complains that when one asks questions about, say, the impenetrability of the soul, whether two spatial souls can occupy the same space, the answers that the soul-theorist is bound to come up with are going to be ad hoc, that is, born out of an interest in preserving dualism rather than in seeking the truth. But here I am persuaded that Kim is assuming that people who accept dualism are those who believe it for religious reasons independent of any rational justification for so believing, perhaps in order to retain their cherished belief in a future life. As he puts it, "We shouldn't do philoso-

---

[11] Jaegwon Kim, "Lonely Souls: Causality and Substance Dualism," in *Soul, Body, and Survival,* ed. Kevin Corcoran (Ithaca, N.Y.: Cornell University Press, 2001), pp. 30-43.

phy by first deciding what we want to prove, or what aims we want to realize, and then posit convenient entities and premises to get us where we want to go."[12] But this need not be so. In this book I have *argued* that we need dualism because if materialism were true the scientific enterprise would not be possible. If that is the case, then if we accept some antimaterialist view, it will be in the interest of making sense of reality and not merely in the interest of propping up this or that religious belief.

Further, Hasker has suggested that even if the soul is not spatial, God could set up a connection between the soul and the body. However, we might ask how the soul identifies the body, given the fact that the physical composition of a body varies with time. Perhaps the body has some identifying characteristic, unique to itself, that it has throughout its career.[13] Or perhaps God not only creates but also sustains the causal interaction between the soul and the body.

Another possibility is Hasker's own emergent dualism, according to which matter in the brain generates the soul. Now I have contended in the previous chapter that it seems implausible to suppose that matter has that capability on naturalistic assumptions, but on theistic assumptions these sorts of capabilities might have been given to matter by God. Nevertheless, even on theistic assumptions, Timothy O'Connor rightly says, "The idea of the natural emergence of a whole substance is a lot to accept."[14] But if that can be accepted (and perhaps given theism its antecedent probability is lessened), then there can be a close relationship between the soul and the body.

One important lesson from this objection is that dualism does not and should not require that the mind exist in radical independence

---

[12]Ibid., p. 42.
[13]This was suggested to me in correspondence with Professor Hasker. However, he does say that the suggestion that the body has a haecceity that the soul recognizes is something of a price to pay to get this account of mind-body interaction going.
[14]Quoted in Hasker, *Emergent Self*, p. 184.

from the physical brain. The dualist should not and need not maintain that the soul is radically independent from the brain. Charles Taliaferro articulates what he calls "integrative dualism." According to integrative dualism, the person is not identical to his or her body. Nonetheless the life of the mind is heavily dependent on the physical brain. Just because the mind is heavily dependent upon the brain does not mean that the mind is nothing but the brain. There are a few alternatives, therefore, to mechanistic materialism, and there are different ways of understanding the relation between the mind and the brain, and the standard objections based on causal interaction are quite simply overrated.[15]

However, a different line of objection comes from adverting to specific recent developments in neurophysiology. Jim Lippard writes that neuroscience makes sense of property dualism but that the works of people such as A. R. Luria, Oliver Sacks and Michael Gazzaniga provide "data about deficits and enhancements in brain function" that are incompatible with substance dualism.[16] One example of this incompatibility is the phenomenon of *visual agnosia*, a condition in which a person who has suffered damage to a particular portion of the brain has trouble processing visual information. What is missing in these cases of brain damage is not the ability to receive visual information, but rather to process that information, a type of activity that, according to Hasker, we should expect a traditional Cartesian dualist to assign to the mind rather than to the brain.[17]

But again I would reiterate the claim that the arguments from reason require only that the account of mental functioning in terms of blind physical processes, operating in accordance with the laws of

---

[15]Charles Taliaferro, *Consciousness and the Mind of God* (Cambridge, Mass.: Cambridge University Press, 1994), pp. 114-22.
[16]Jim Lippard, "Historical but Indistinguishable Differences: Some Notes on Victor Reppert's Paper," *Philo* 2 (spring-summer 1999): 49.
[17]Hasker, *Emergent Self*, pp. 154-55.

physics rather than in accordance with the laws of logic, cannot be comprehensive. It seems to me to be perfectly compatible with an extensive dependence of the mind on the physical brain; it only says that if mechanistic accounts of rational inference are the only accounts you can get out of brain science, then a neurophysiological account cannot be causally complete.

Another line of objection claims that since we know that human beings, and therefore their minds, are a product of biological evolution, and since we also know that that evolutionary process is physical, we must therefore conclude that the mind is nothing over and above the physical brain. As Paul Churchland puts it:

> Most scientists and philosophers would cite the presumed fact that humans have their origin in 4.5 billion years of chemical and biological evolution as a weighty consideration of expecting mental phenomena to be nothing but a particularly exquisite articulation of the basic properties of matter and energy.[18]

Or again Colin McGinn: "Consider the universe before conscious beings came along: the odds did not look good that such beings could come to exist. The world was all just physical objects and physical forces, devoid of life."[19]

Of course the epistemic status of evolutionary biology is, to say the least, a highly controversial topic. I would just insist that when we hear triumphalistic claims about evolution as an established fact (where the claim is that the nonintelligent forces of random mutation and natural selection comprise a comprehensive explanation for how all species developed), it is important to distinguish five different claims, all of which are presented as "evolution," while their denials are referred to as "creationist." The "five points of evolutionism" are as follows:

---

[18]Paul Churchland, *The Engine of Reason, the Seat of the Soul* (Cambridge, Mass.: MIT Press, 1995), p. 211.
[19]Colin McGinn, *The Mysterious Flame: Conscious Minds in a Material World* (New York: Basic Books, 1999), p. 14

1. The universe has been in existence for a very long time, and the earth, while young relative to the age of the universe, is nevertheless about 4 billion years old.

2. Species emerged progressively throughout geological time.

3. All of life emerged from a common ancestor, the first one-celled living thing that came into being millions of years ago.

4. The entire speciation process, the transitions from one species to another, happened naturalistically, without supernatural intervention.

5. Life itself emerged through a natural process (i.e., the sun working on the primordial soup) without supernatural intervention.[20]

Now I am inclined to suppose that the first two claims have been firmly established by scientific evidence; to accept "young earth" and "young universe" creationism would be to say that the universe is around six thousand years old; but there are stars in existence which are evidently millions of light years away. Clearly the denial of the first two points of evolution would involve rejecting claims that have the strongest of scientific warrant. Denial of the last two points, on the other hand, seems to be consistent with what we know scientifically. The arguments from reason are creationist in a *very* limited sense, requiring only that our capacity to reason is not entirely the product of blind processes. Lewis, clearly, is open to the possibility of evolutionary processes being involved in the development of reason:

> But the theist need not, and does not, grant these terms. He is not committed to the view that reason is a comparatively recent develop-

---

[20]Alvin Plantinga, "When Faith and Reason Clash: Evolution and the Bible," *Christian Scholar's Review* 21 (1991): 8-33. The phrase "the five points of evolutionism" is mine, but unfortunately I am unable to supply a suitable acronym corresponding to TULIP, which is used for the five points of Calvinism. An anonymous reviewer for this book suggested a sixth point, that the "the laws of physics and initial conditions were not intelligently configured to produce a specific outcome." This sixth point makes evolutionism explicitly atheistic.

ment moulded by a process of selection which can select only the biologically useful. For him reason—the reason of God—is older than Nature, and from it the orderliness of Nature, which alone enables us to know her, is derived. For him, the human mind in the act of knowing is illuminated by the Divine mind. It is set free, in the measure required, from the huge nexus of non-rational causation; free from this to be determined by the truth known. And the preliminary processes within Nature which led up to this liberation, if there were any, were designed to do so.[21]

Sometimes it is argued that the long history of scientific success gives us warrant in believing that whatever we cannot explain in a physicalistic manner now should not be regarded as something that cannot be given a physicalistic explanation; rather we should simply regard difficulties for scientific explanation as temporary difficulties to be overcome someday by further progress. Indeed, the arguments from reason are often criticized as appeals to ignorance. All that versions of the argument from reason could show would be that an explanation has not been provided, not that an explanation could not be provided. Given the prestige of naturalistic science, these versions of the argument from reason are simply not an adequate reason for rejecting naturalism. Rather, a kind of "promissory materialism" is recommended. Nicholas Tattersall, for example, maintains that Lewis commits the fallacy of assuming that if we cannot explain why something is true, we are unjustified in believing that it is true. On the contrary, we know that grass is green, or that water expands when it freezes, without knowing why grass is green or why water expands when it freezes.[22]

But the problem with naturalism and reasoning is not simply that we do not happen to know the physical explanation for reason.

[21]Lewis, *Miracles*, pp. 22-23.
[22]Nicholas Tattersall, "A Critique of C. S. Lewis's *Miracles*," The Secular Web, Modern Library (2000) <www.infidels.org/library/modern/nicholas_tattersall/miracles.html>.

It is that naturalism, with its claim that purpose and intentionality are not fundamental to the universe, gives us a prima facie reason to believe that reasoning should not exist. Yet its existence cannot be denied without undermining the very scientific enterprise from which naturalism gains its support. And attempts to account for the existence of reason naturalistically invariably fail to explain reasoning naturalistically; rather, they surreptitiously "sneak in" the very concepts they are trying to explain through the back door. As Darek Barefoot argues:

> Tattersall also says Lewis blunders in failing to acknowledge that we can believe even that which we understand imperfectly. We may not understand why the grass is green, but we don't on that basis question that it is green. Tattersall here confuses logical absurdity with phenomena incompletely known. To learn why grass is green simply involves gathering more information. To learn how non-rational processes give rise to rational thought is like learning how a three-dimensional object can be created by arranging lines on a two-dimensional surface. We need not draw lines all day long in every geometric pattern imaginable to realize that the task is impossible. It is true that by means of perspective drawing we can usefully represent a three-dimensional shape, such as a cube, in two dimensions, just as human reason can be represented and communicated usefully by computer programs and even by humbler devices such as multiplication charts and slide rules. Nevertheless, we can identify a set of lines in two dimensions as representing a cube only because we occupy three-dimensional space, and similarly we can appreciate that the blind functions of a computer have been so arranged as to accomplish a rational purpose only because, unlike the computer, we possess genuine rationality.[23]

Naturalistic philosophers of mind often quite honestly acknowledge the philosophical difficulties surrounding the problems of con-

---

[23]Darek Barefoot, "A Response to Nicholas Tattersall's 'A Critique of *Miracles* by C. S. Lewis,'" The Secular Web Kiosk (2001) <http://www.secweb.org/asset.asp?AssetID=89>.

sciousness and reasoning. Jerry Fodor says, "Nobody has the slightest idea how anything material could be conscious. Nobody even knows what it would be like to have the slightest idea of how anything material could be conscious."[24] Ned Block maintains:

> We have no conception of our physical or functional nature that allows us to understand how it could explain our subjective experience. ... [I]n the case of consciousness we have nothing—zilch—worthy of being called a research program, nor are there any substantive proposals about how to go about starting one. Researchers are stumped.[25]

Of course there is scientific research going on about the nature of consciousness, and the achievements of these enterprises should not be denied or underestimated. But do these research programs provide an actual scientific explanation of how changes in matter give rise to subjective experience? What we often find in many cases is a subtle changing of the subject from conscious experience to something that can be described and analyzed mechanistically. If consciousness is re-described in input-output terms, then of course one can say that consciousness is being explained. The danger, however, is that consciousness will not be explained, but rather explained away, that is, explained in such a way that what we ordinarily think of as consciousness is re-described for the sake of better scientific tractability. If we make it clear that what we are talking about is the inner subjective state of thinking or feeling or seeing something, then I believe that these philosophers' puzzlement as to how research can proceed reflects the sober truth of the matter.

But shouldn't naturalistic science be given the benefit of every doubt in dealing with explanatory difficulties? Since the history of science is a history of a triumph of naturalistic explanation, perhaps

---

[24]Jerry A. Fodor, "The Big Idea: Can There Be a Science of the Mind," *Times Literary Supplement*, July 3, 1992, p. 5.

[25]Ned Block, "Consciousness," in *A Companion to the Philosophy of Mind*, ed. Sam Guttenplan (Oxford: Blackwell, 1994), p. 211.

we should give naturalism the benefit of whatever doubts might be posed by the arguments from reason.

But is the history of science really the triumph of this kind of mechanistic materialism? Naturalists today typically accommodate the doctrines of microphysical indeterminism and even an absolute beginning of the universe to their naturalistic philosophy. But before these doctrines became widely accepted in the scientific community, it was thought that the denial of these doctrines had to be presupposed by the scientific enterprise. A genuinely "naturalistic" world-view was perforce deterministic and denied the possibility of the universe having a beginning. Such "presuppositions" of science should be seriously questioned, especially if, as I have argued, these presuppositions undermine the possible existence of scientists.

OBJECTIONS BASED ON MYSTERIES CONCERNING GOD

Dennett maintains that unless we analyze reason and intentionality in terms of that which is not rational and not intentional, then we are offering a question-begging account of these phenomena. Hence, whatever puzzles arise from explaining the mind materialistically, moving to a nonmaterialist worldview only puts the problem one step back. If one rejects a naturalistic answer to the question "Why is rational inference possible in a naturalistic universe?" and instead appeals to the existence of a rational God, can we not ask, "Why is God rational?" and be back where we started?[26]

But I would argue that Dennett's insistence is itself question-begging. It is supposed that it is God's nature to be rational. If we explain one thing in terms of something else, and that something else in terms of something else again, the chain of explanation will have to terminate somewhere, and the theist explains the existence of ra-

---

[26]Daniel Dennett, "Why the Law of Effect Will Not Go Away," in *Brainstorms: Philosophical Essays on Mind and Psychology* (Cambridge, Mass.: MIT Press, 1977), pp. 44-45.

tionality in the universe by appealing to the inherent rationality of God. The materialist cannot actually argue that one ought never to explain anything in terms of something having such and such a nature. For example, a materialist would explain that my heart is in the right place not because of any divine design but because creatures with hearts in the wrong place died before passing on their genes. One cannot go on giving reductive explanations forever. If, as I have argued, we have good reason to suppose that reason cannot be built up out of nonintentional and nonteleological building blocks, then in order to preserve reason and the logical foundations of science, we have good reason to accept a nonmaterialist understanding of the universe. Explaining reason in terms of the inherent rationality of God is no more question-begging than explaining physical states in terms of prior physical states. If the foregoing argument is correct, then explaining reason in terms of unreason explains reason away and undercuts the very reason on which the explanation is supposed to be based.

Drange objects, in his debate with Douglas Wilson, that an adequate form of the argument from reason, if it is used to support belief in the existence of God, must confront some questions concerning the nature of God before it can be thought of as actually supporting theism. In particular:

1. Does God transcend logic as well as space and time?

2. What does it mean to be created in the image of the transcendent God?

3. How can a being who is outside time do any thinking or creating at all? Thinking and creating, as we understand them, both involve time.

4. Did God create time itself? If so, how is that possible? Did he exist *before* time?

5. How exactly does God create things? We need to understand this in order to explain anything by appeal to God's creative activity. If it is claimed that God's nature or methods are beyond human comprehension, then how can it be an *adequate* explanation . . . to appeal to God's creative activity to try to account for rational thought? Such a hypothesis needs to be clearly understood to have any value *as an explanation.*

6. Did God first create the universe and then wait ten billion years before creating life on earth and then another three billion years before creating humans? If so, how come? If (as Wilson claimed) God created things for his own glory, then why did he wait so long between the creation of the universe and the creation of beings capable of glorifying him? Also, why is it that there are not more planets in the universe containing beings who glorify God, seeing that that was his purpose? Our planet is like a speck of dust in the Pacific Ocean. Why did God make the universe so big if all he was interested in was us?[27]

Taking these questions in succession, I would answer (1) by saying that God does not transcend logic; rather, rationality is part of God's essence. While material particles, being material, cannot be essentially rational, it makes perfect sense to say that God is essentially a rational being. In answer to (2), what it means to be created in the image of a transcendent God, at least as far as this discussion is concerned, is to have the power to perceive rational connections, what Lewis called ground-and-consequent relations. It no doubt means more than that, but it does not mean less. In answer to (3), the argument from reason, as I have presented it, does not require that God be outside of time.

---

[27]Theodore Drange, "First Rebuttal." It should be noted that Drange in this debate was arguing against what is known as the transcendental argument for God or TAG, developed in large part by Cornelius Van Til and Gregory Bahnsen. It bears some similarities to the argument from reason as I am presenting it, but is also different in other respects. It seems to me that in that debate Wilson did not respond adequately to Drange's objections.

Some advocates of the argument, like Lewis, are atemporalists with respect to the nature of God, others, like Hasker, are not. The argument is neutral with respect to temporalist-atemporalist debate, and so difficulties for atemporalism are not objections to the argument unless problems for a temporalist view of God can also be advanced. Neither is the argument from reason committed to the idea in (4) that God created time, a claim that would be denied by a temporalist like Hasker. As to how God created things (5), does it really make sense to ask an omnipotent being how he (or she) created something? If the creation of the universe is a coherent possibility, and God is omnipotent, then we know it is possible for God to create the universe. Finally, with regard to (6), while we know that God was interested in creating the human race, we surely do not know whether God was only interested in creating humans, or whether God created Vulcans, Klingons and Ferengi as well, or whether God created only one universe, or why God created one exactly this size as opposed to a larger or a smaller one. It is not as if energy or time is a scarce resource for God and we have to ask him, if he seems to be "wasting" it, why he isn't putting it to better use. "Waste" is an issue only where there is scarcity.

SCIENTIFIC FIDEISM

I recognize that, for many people, it is not merely the case that naturalism is true, naturalism serves as a fundamental core belief that controls what can even be considered. We often find religious believers who seem to be almost totally resistant to anything that calls their beliefs into question. I am inclined to suppose that something like that is going on in people like Richard Lewontin:

> Our willingness to accept scientific claims that are against common sense is the key to an understanding of the real struggle between science and the supernatural. We take the side of science in spite of its failure to fulfill many of its extravagant promises of health and life, in spite of the tolerance of the scientific community of unsubstantiated just-so stories,

because we have a prior commitment, commitment to materialism. It is not that the methods and institutions of science somehow compel us to accept a material explanation of the phenomenal world, but on the contrary, that we are forced by our a priori adherence to material causes to create an apparatus of investigation and a set of concepts that produce material causes, no matter how counterintuitive, no matter how mystifying to the uninitiated. Moreover, that materialism is absolute, for we cannot allow a Divine Foot in the door. The eminent Kant scholar Lewis Beck used to say that anyone who believes in God can believe in anything. To appeal to an omnipotent deity is to allow that at any moment the regularities of nature may be ruptured, the Miracles may happen.[28]

This seems to me to clearly be a scientific form of fideism, in which the foundational claims of materialism cannot be questioned. I do not think the arguments from reason—or any other arguments—can dislodge this kind of fideism.

On the other hand, we can easily imagine how this sort of fideism would sound to most of us if it were directed toward anything but science. Suppose someone were to make this sort of claim on behalf of, say, the inerrancy of Scripture:

Our willingness to accept biblical teachings that are against common sense is the key to an understanding of the real struggle between faith and unbelief. We take the side of Scripture in spite of its failure to fulfill many of its extravagant promises of health and life, in spite of the existence of unsubstantiated just-so stories in Scripture, because we have a prior commitment, a commitment to Scripture's inerrancy. It is not that the methods and institutions of biblical study somehow compel us to accept only interpretations that are in accordance with the Bible's inerrancy, but on the contrary, that we are forced by our a priori adherence to biblical inerrancy to create a method of biblical study

---

[28] Richard Lewontin, "Billions and Billions of Demons," review of *The Demon-Haunted World: Science as a Candle in the Dark* by Carl Sagan, *New York Review of Books*, January 9, 1997, pp. 28-32.

that produces explanations that are consistent with inerrancy, no matter how counterintuitive, no matter how mystifying to the uninitiated.
Moreover, our commitment to inerrancy is absolute, for we cannot allow doubt to get its foot in the door. For anyone capable of doubting
the Word of God in any respect will end up doubting it in all respects.

Such a statement, coming from a Christian theologian, would no
doubt prompt many to use the term *fundamentalist* as a term of
abuse. Timothy Erdel labels Lewontin's skepticism as dishonest skepticism. He writes:

> The "dishonesty" is not a lack of candor. The statement could scarcely
> be plainer or more straightforward, and Lewontin is to be com-
> mended for the clarity with which he states his view. Rather, the "dis-
> honesty" is in the absolute refusal to consider alternatives, to
> predetermine that all scientific questions will be considered within
> certain clearly prescribed limits for the explicit prior use of defending
> those same limits. The matter is not simply one of begging the ques-
> tion or of circular reasoning (to reason at all requires some point of
> view), but of vicious rigidity, since nothing empirical or theoretical
> can ever modify the presupposition of materialism. It is also "dishon-
> est" because anyone who assumed a different metaphysical starting
> point with the same sort of rigidity, for example, that the universe is
> filled with "billions and billions of demons" (Lewontin's own play on
> two titles by Sagan) would be rightfully scorned by Lewontin.[29]

Now I do believe that a certain amount of tenacity in the face of
apparently contrary evidence is necessary for anyone who holds to a
worldview. However, when one insists on padlocking one's belief system against the possibility of evidence that the belief system might be
in error, I am inclined to suspect that all is not well from the point of
view of rationality. In the case of naturalists, I suspect that what

---

[29]Timothy Erdel, "The Rationality of Christian Faith" (Ph.D. diss., University of Illinois at
Urbana-Champaign, 2000), p. 83.

Thomas Nagel calls the fear of religion is perhaps at work. Nagel forthrightly attributes this fear to himself when he says,

> In speaking of the fear of religion, I don't mean to refer to the entirely reasonable hostility toward certain established religions and religious institutions, in virtue of their objectionable moral doctrines, social policies, and political influence. Nor am I referring to the association of many religious beliefs with superstition and the acceptance of evident empirical falsehoods. I am talking about something deeper—namely, the fear of religion itself. I speak from experience, being strongly subject to this fear myself: I want atheism to be true and am made uneasy by the fact that some of the most intelligent and well-informed people I know are religious believers. It isn't just that I don't believe in God, and, naturally, hope that I'm right about my belief. It's that I hope there is no God! I don't want there to be a God; I don't want the universe to be like that.[30]

I want to stress that, with respect to the question of God, I am not saying that all the ulterior motives are on one side. Believers are accustomed to people like Marx and Freud accusing them of wishful thinking. Christians are told that we want to believe in a happy afterlife for ourselves and that this prevents us from soberly assessing the evidence for and against the existence of God. Most people have some desire or other as to what they hope will be the truth about God, either they hope or fear that God exists, and some of us have both hope and fear. Lewis reports (and we have no reason to disbelieve him) that believing in God and in an afterlife was the last thing he wanted to believe, and when he came to believe he was the most reluctant convert in all England. He also said that God fulfilled his deepest longing. So it is surely possible for one and the same person to have a desire both to believe and to disbelieve.

As a refutation of an opposing position, coming up with ulterior motives for one's opponents' beliefs commits the ad hominem fal-

---

[30]Thomas Nagel, *The Last Word* (Oxford: Oxford University Press, 1997), p. 130.

lacy. But one should be conscious of the nonrational motivations that one might have for believing something. Everyone who tries to think, if they are honest with themselves, will be aware of the impact that various kinds of desire have on belief. No one is perfectly rational, and it is easier to see irrationality in one's intellectual opponents than in oneself. But when someone attempts to padlock their beliefs against the possibility of even considering an opposing viewpoint, I am inclined to suspect that ulterior motives are at work.

Nevertheless, a person's decision concerning what worldview is true is invariably decided by a variety of factors, and the story of Lewis's own conversion is certainly a story of a number of converging considerations working together to persuade him to become a Christian. So I am not going to defend the claim that the arguments from reason close the case against naturalism. Nor do I seek to show that any naturalist who pays attention to these arguments can remain a naturalist only at the cost of patent irrationality. Single arguments are rarely sufficient to bring about a worldview change in reasonable people.

However, I contend that the arguments from reason do provide some substantial reasons for preferring theism to naturalism. The "problem of reason" is a huge problem for naturalism, as serious or, I would say, more serious, than the problem of evil is for theists. But while theists have expended considerable effort in confronting the problem of evil, the problem of reason has not as yet been acknowledged as a serious problem for naturalism.

C. S. Lewis's dangerous idea is the idea that if we explain reason naturalistically we shall end up explaining it away, that is, explaining it in such a way that it cannot serve as a foundation for the natural sciences that are themselves the foundation for naturalism. As I hope this book has shown, this constitutes an extremely powerful reason to reject naturalism and to accept some other worldview that makes reason fundamental to reality.

Bibliography

Adams, Robert M. *The Virtue of Faith and Other Essays in Philosophical Theology.* New York: Oxford University Press, 1987.

Anscombe, G. E. M. *Metaphysics and the Philosophy of Mind.* Vol. 2 of *The Collected Papers of G. E. M. Anscombe,* 3 vols. Minneapolis: University of Minnesota Press, 1981.

Balfour, Arthur. *The Foundations of Belief: Notes Introductory to the Study of Theology,* 8th ed. New York: Longmans, 1906.

———. *Theism and Humanism.* New York: Hodder & Stoughton, 1915.

Beversluis, John. *C. S. Lewis and the Search for Rational Religion.* Grand Rapids, Mich.: Eerdmans, 1985.

Drange, Theodore. "Reply to Reppert." *Philosophia Christi* 5, no. 1 (2003).

Hasker, William. *The Emergent Self.* Ithaca, N.Y.: Cornell University Press, 1999.

———. "What About a Sensible Naturalism?" *Philosophia Christi* 5, no. 1 (2003).

Kim, Jaegwon. *Supervenience and Mind: Selected Philosophical Essays.* Cambridge: Cambridge University Press, 1991.

Lewis, C. S. *Christian Reflections.* Edited with an introduction by Walter Hooper. Grand Rapids, Mich.: Eerdmans, 1967.

———. *A Grief Observed.* New York: Seabury, 1963.

———. *Miracles: A Preliminary Study.* Rev. ed. New York: Macmillan, 1978.

Lippard, Jim. "Historical but Indistinguishable Differences: Some Notes on Victor Reppert's Paper." *Philo* 2, no. 1 (1999).

Nagel, Thomas. *The Last Word.* Oxford: Oxford University Press, 1997.

Parsons, Keith. "Defending Objectivity." *Philo* 2, no. 1 (1999).

———. "Further Reflections on the Argument from Reason." *Philo* 3, no. 1 (2000).

———. "Need Reasons by Causes? A Further Reply to Victor Reppert's Argument from Reason." *Philosophia Christi* 5, no. 1 (2003).

Plantinga, Alvin. *Warrant and Proper Function.* Oxford: Oxford University Press, 1993.

———.*Warranted Christian Belief.* Oxford: Oxford University Press, 2000.

Reppert, Victor. "The Argument from Reason." Posted online at <www. infidels.org/library/modern/victor_reppert/reason.html>. Subsequently published in *Philo* 2, no. 1 (1999).

———. "Causal Closure, Mechanism and Rational Inference." *Philosophia Christi*, 2nd ser., 3, no. 2 (2001).

———. "The Lewis-Anscombe Controversy: A Discussion of the Issues." *Christian Scholar's Review* 19, no. 3 (1989).

———. *Physical Causes and Rational Belief: A Problem for Materialism?* Ph.D diss., University of Illinois at Urbana-Champaign, 1989, UMI no. 9010997.

———. "Reply to Drange, Parsons, and Hasker." *Philosophia Christi*, 2nd ser., 5, no. 1 (2003).

———. "Reply to Parsons and Lippard on the Argument from Reason." *Philo* 2, no. 1 (2000).

———. "Several Formulations of the Argument from Reason." *Philosophia Christi*, 2nd ser., 5, no. 1 (2003).

Index